ebox Guide

ANCIENT
BRITAIN

This book describes places to visit throughout Britain which display fascinating evidence of life and death in prehistoric times. The sites, dotted across the landscape from Cornwall to the Scottish islands, range from mysterious standing stones to burial mounds, lofty hillforts to cave dwellings. The story of Britain's prehistory from earliest times up to the coming of the Romans is told in the book's introduction and through the descriptions of the sites themselves. Details are also given of museums, societies and organisations specialising in archaeology.

The book is divided into six geographic regions. Within each region, the places to visit are listed in alphabetical order.

About the author

Timothy Darvill was educated in Cheltenham and at Southampton University where he obtained an honours degree in archaeology. His postgraduate research focused on the Neolithic period in Wales and the mid-west of England. He has directed a number of excavations, and was Secretary of the Committee for Archaeology in Gloucestershire between 1980 and 1985. A Member of the Institute of Field Archaeologists and a Fellow of the Society of Antiquaries, Dr Darvill is a part-time tutor in archaeology for the Department of Extra-Mural Studies at Bristol University and a freelance archaeological consultant. He has written several books on prehistoric Britain, including work for English Heritage.

Acknowledgements

The publishers gratefully acknowledge the following for the use of their photographs. Many of the photographs were supplied by Mick Sharp (designated MS in following credits), Cambridge University Collection of Air Photographs (CU) and Janet and Colin Bord (JCB). When more than one photograph appears on a page, credits are listed top to bottom.
7. Both MS **8.** CU **9.** Oxford Radiocarbon Accelerator Unit **13.** MS **15.** AA Picture Library **17.** Royal Museum of Scotland **18.** Michael Holford **19.** All AA Picture Library **20.** MS **21.** JCB **23.** MS **24.** CU **26.** JCB **27.** CU **30.** JCB, CU **31.** MS **32.** JCB **33.** MS **34.** Both MS **35.** CU **37.** F. Gibson, AA Picture Library **38.** Somerset Levels Trust (inset), Michael Holford **39.** AA Picture Library **40.** AA Picture Library, S and O Mathews **41.** MS **42.** JCB **43, 44.** Both MS **45.** Ashmolean Museum, Oxford **46.** MS **47.** CU **48.** JCB **50.** CU, MS **51.** JCB **52.** Timothy Darvill, JCB **54.** S and O Mathews **55.** JCB **56, 57.** Both MS **58.** MS, National Museum of Wales **59.** MS **60.** Both Flag Fen Trust **61.** MS, JCB **64.** JCB **65, 66, 67.** All MS **68.** JCB **70, 71.** Both Timothy Darvill **72, 73.** Both MS **74.** JCB **77.** Timothy Darvill (top left), MS (top right), National Museum of Wales **78.** MS, B Johnson **79.** JCB **80.** B Johnson **82.** AA Picture Library **83.** CU **84.** JCB **85.** MS **86.** CU , JCB **87, 88.** MS **89, 90, 91, 92.** All JCB **93.** E A Bowness **94.** CU **95, 96.** JCB **97.** MS **99.** CU **100.** MS, CU **102, 103.** MS **104.** JCB, MS **105, 106.** MS **107.** Both JCB **108.** JCB, MS **110.** Both MS **111.** Both JCB **112.** MS **114, 115.** Both MS.

AA

Glovebox Guide

ANCIENT BRITAIN

Timothy Darvill

Produced by the Publishing Division
of The Automobile Association

4

Editor: *Roger Thomas*
Art Editor: *Harry Williams FCSD*
Cover illustration: *David Sim*
Typesetting: *Afal, Cardiff*
Printing: *Purnell Book Production Ltd, a member of the
        BPCC Group*

The publishers also wish to acknowledge the following as
sources of reference material. This material has been redrawn
and appears in the form of illustrations/maps on the pages
indicated.

9. *Guide to Devizes Museum* (Wiltshire Archaeological and
Natural History Society, 1964) **22.** *The Avebury Monuments,*
Vatcher and Vatcher (English Heritage, 1976) **32.** *Norton
Fitzwarren Site Guide* (Somerset County Council, 1985) **36.**
Cornish Archaeology, Volume 13 (Cornwall Archaeological
Society, 1974) **51.** *The Medway Megaliths,* Philp and Dutto
(Kent Archaeological Trust, 1985) **54.*** *Hertfordshire
Archaeology, Volume 8* (St Albans and Hertfordshire
Archaeological Society, 1982) **62.** *Culture and Environment,*
Foster and Alcock (Routledge and Kegan Paul, 1963)
65. *Gwernvale and Penywyrlod,* Britnell and Savory (Cambrian
Archaeological Association, 1984) **81.** *Survey of
Northamptonshire* (Royal Commission on the Historic
Monuments of England, 1983) **93.** *The Stone Circles of the
British Isles,* Burl (Yale University Press, 1976) **109.*** *Jarlshof
Site Guide* (HMSO, 1966).

*** Originally based on Ordnance Survey mapping with
permission of HMSO. Crown copyright reserved.

Produced by the Publishing Division of
The Automobile Association

Distributed in the United Kingdom by the
Publishing Division of The Automobile Association,
Fanum House, Basingstoke, Hampshire RG21 2EA

The contents of this publication are believed correct
at the time of printing. Nevertheless, the Publishers
cannot accept responsibility for errors or omissions,
nor for changes in details given.

ISBN 0 86145 683 1

AA Ref 51460

Published by The Automobile Association

ANCIENT BRITAIN

Contents

Introduction 6
  A Wealth of Sites 6
  Discovering the Prehistoric Past 8
  Britain Before the Romans 10
  Using this Book 16

Places to Visit
  The West Country 21
  South and South-East England 43
  Wales 55
  Central England and East Anglia 73
  The North Country 89
  Scotland 101

Sites with Restricted Opening 116
Museums to Visit 116
Further Reading 117
Joining In 117
Glossary 118
Index 119

A collection of Mesolithic artefacts

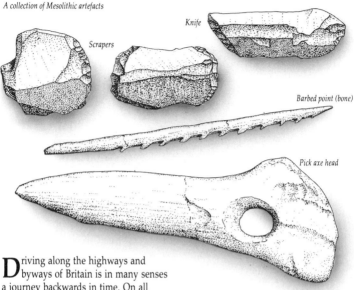

Knife

Scrapers

Barbed point (bone)

Pick axe head

Driving along the highways and byways of Britain is in many senses a journey backwards in time. On all sides, and sometimes even under the road itself, there are fragments of our ancient past side by side with the modern. Medieval villages, old churches, Saxon crosses and Roman villas are commonplace, but far older still, and equally abundant, are the barrows, hillforts, stone circles, camps, standing stones and other relics of prehistoric times. This book is all about these very ancient remains, the prehistoric sites which date from the time between the first appearance of people in Britain during the last Ice Age over 500,000 years ago and the Roman Conquest which took place in AD43.

A WEALTH OF SITES

Prehistoric sites range in size from small cairns of stone resulting from the clearance of fields for cultivation through to massive sacred enclosures like the henge at Avebury, Wiltshire.

They vary in their visibility from low banks forming the boundaries of fields to elaborate standing structures like the circles and alignments at Callanish, Lewis, or the great standing stone at Rudston, Humberside, which towers to a height of 7.7m. Some monuments, like Stonehenge, Wiltshire, are unique; others, like the round barrows of Bronze Age times, were constructed in vast numbers. All monuments, large or small, modest or imposing, unique or commonplace, tell us something of the story of Britain's past. The aim here is to describe a selection of the best-known and most important sites which illustrate the homes, farms, work places, burial grounds and ceremonial centres of our distant ancestors.

Most prehistoric monuments in Britain are found in the countryside, crowning hilltops, nestling in quiet valleys, sprawling across open moorland or lurking in dark woods. This is not because the areas which are now towns and cities were unsuitable places for prehistoric communities to live in, but simply a result of dense occupation in recent times which has either buried the prehistoric sites deep beneath the pavements and buildings or destroyed them when foundations and service trenches were dug. Even the prehistoric sites in the countryside do not escape the pressures of modern life, and it is salutary to remember that throughout Britain monuments are being lost every day through intensive agriculture, forestry, new road schemes, industrial development, land reclamation, quarrying and urban expansion.

Some of the prehistoric monuments listed in this book are managed as tourist attractions, and while they may be easy to reach and provided with car parks, toilets and gift shops, they frequently lose something of their atmosphere and mystery as a result. Others, probably the majority, are not managed in this way and are in a sense more authentic because they are uncluttered by the trappings of modern life. These sites can be slightly more difficult to find, but the rewards of visiting them are great.

The ancient monuments described in this book are divided into six regional groups: the West Country; South and South-East England; Wales; Central England and East Anglia; the North Country; and Scotland. Within these regions the sites are listed alphabetically, and the map at the beginning of each section indicates the approximate position of each place to visit.

An Iron Age hillfort of about 400BC crowns St Catherine's Hill near Winchester

Some areas of Britain are so rich in prehistoric remains that even within the space of a few miles there is a great deal to see. Twelve such areas have been included here, and these make ideal destinations for a day out or a short holiday. Exploring the prehistoric sites described in this book will take you to some of the finest countryside and most impressive scenery in Britain.

The Bronze Age Druids' Circle, high in the hills above Penmaenmawr

As a background to the monuments you will see, the following three sections briefly describe how we discover the prehistoric past, the social, technological and climatic changes that took place during prehistory, and how to use this book when visiting prehistoric monuments. Following the six regional sections there are four short sections providing notes on sites with restricted opening, a list of museums to visit, a selection of further reading, and information about how to follow up an interest in prehistoric archaeology as a pastime or hobby.

In preparing this book, technical terms have been avoided wherever possible, but those that have been used are fully explained in a comprehensive **glossary** near the very end of the book (pages 118—19).

The fun of visiting ancient sites, of course, begins when you start looking at the monuments themselves. This book tells you a little of what is known about their history, purpose, date and any special features to look out for. The rest is up to you!

DISCOVERING THE PREHISTORIC PAST

Finding out about the prehistoric past involves three main steps: identifying and recording sites; investigating sites; and analysing and interpreting the results of the first two stages.

Many sites are identified through field surveys where, by careful examination of the landscape with the eye of experience, the characteristic shapes of burial mounds, enclosures, fieldsystems, standing stones and so on can be recognised. Where land has been heavily cultivated, additional evidence

may be gathered by methodically scanning ploughed fields and recording any flints, unusual stone, or pottery which has been brought to the surface. Chance finds of pottery, flint or metalwork which come to light during the construction of a new road or through some other activity that disturbs the ground are also important, and sometimes provide the first indication of a previously unknown site.

A technique of discovery that extends the power of the human eye is aerial photography. In winter, earthworks can be identified and recorded by the careful use of low-angle sunlight or by a light sprinkling of snow to accentuate shadows. In spring, and again in late summer, differential crop growth over infilled ditches or pits can sometimes be seen clearly from high above. And in autumn, slight changes in

An aerial view of one of the three Thornborough Circles, North Yorkshire

the colour and texture of the soil indicating the position of burial mounds, old buildings or ramparts may be revealed after a field has been ploughed.

The investigation of prehistoric sites is altogether more complicated than their identification and recording. Various electronic sensing devices are available which can, as it were, look through the soil to see what lies beneath, but these provide no substitute

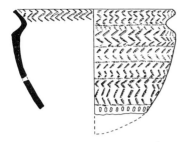

Late Neolithic pot from Wiltshire (after Annable and Simpson 1964)

for excavation as a way of really unearthing details of what actually took place at a particular site.

Modern excavations aim to examine, systematically, one layer or deposit within a site at a time in order to build up a picture of the way buried structures and objects relate to one another. This in turn leads to an understanding of the activities that took place on the site, where rubbish was dumped, where food was prepared, where people slept, where the animals were kept, and so on.

After an excavation, the work of sorting out, analysing and interpreting the finds begins. This is less glamorous than the digging itself, but is essential for a complete understanding of the site. Human skeletons are aged and sexed, the animals from which bones have come are identified, and any pottery, flint tools, stone implements and metalwork are examined to see how they were made and used. Scientific studies provide information about the sources of raw materials used by prehistoric communities and the level of their technological abilities.

Pollen, snail shells, fragments of tiny insects, seeds and pieces of plant matter extracted from samples of soil collected during an excavation help to provide a picture of the vegetation, animal populations and the general environment within and around the site.

Radiocarbon dating is the most reliable way of determining the age of a site, and it works by measuring the amount of radioactive carbon 14 in samples of bone, charcoal or wood. While they are alive, all plants and animals absorb minute quantities of carbon 14 from the atmosphere, but when they die no further carbon 14 can be taken in, and what is already present begins to decay very slowly (about half will have disappeared after 5,568 years).

The Oxford Radiocarbon Accelerator Unit, which measures radioactive carbon 14

The rate of decay is fairly even, and so by finding out the concentration of carbon 14 remaining in an ancient sample it is possible to calculate how much time has elapsed since the plant or animal died, and hence its age.

By piecing together information from chance finds, field surveys, aerial photographs, explorations with electronic sensing devices, excavations and post-excavation analysis, it is possible to reconstruct a picture of Britain's changing environment and the communities who lived here in the centuries before the Romans arrived.

BRITAIN BEFORE THE ROMANS

Exactly when people first settled in Britain is uncertain, but it was probably between a quarter and a half a million years ago, during a warm period in the middle of the Pleistocene Ice Age.

Prehistory therefore spans a very long time, and for this reason is traditionally divided into five main periods: Palaeolithic/Old Stone Age before 10,000BC, Mesolithic/Middle Stone Age (10,000—4400BC), Neolithic/New Stone Age (4400—2500BC), Bronze Age (2500—800BC) and Iron Age (800BC—AD50).

PALAEOLITHIC AND MESOLITHIC HUNTERS

The last Ice Age involved at least four main expansions of the polar ice cap, between which were episodes of glacial retreat when much of Europe had an almost equatorial climate. During these warm periods small bands of people visited what is now Britain while pursuing herds of wild horse, deer, bison, wild cattle and elephant. For much of the time Britain was simply a peninsula of mainland Europe so groups could roam far and wide.

These early visitors were a primitive species of Man known as *Homo erectus*, the stone tools and weapons they used being known as the Acheulian toolmaking tradition. By about 100,000BC, however, the human population and the kinds of tools they used had changed. *Homo erectus* was succeeded by *Homo neanderthalensis* (Neanderthal Man) and the characteristic equipment of these communities belongs to what is known as the Mousterian tradition. These people sometimes lived in caves, as around the Cheddar Gorge

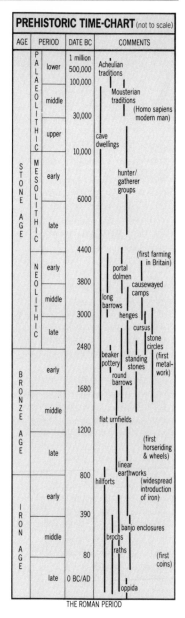

PREHISTORIC TIME-CHART (not to scale)

AGE	PERIOD	DATE BC	COMMENTS
STONE AGE	PALAEOLITHIC lower	1 million / 500,000 / 100,000	Acheulian traditions
	PALAEOLITHIC middle	30,000	Mousterian traditions (Homo sapiens modern man)
	PALAEOLITHIC upper	10,000	cave dwellings
	MESOLITHIC early	6000	hunter/gatherer groups
	MESOLITHIC late	4400	(first farming in Britain)
	NEOLITHIC early	3800	portal dolmen / causewayed camps
	NEOLITHIC middle	3000	long barrows / henges
	NEOLITHIC late	2480	cursus / stone circles
BRONZE AGE	early	1680	beaker pottery / standing stones / round barrows / (first metalwork)
	middle	1200	flat urnfields
	late	800	(first horseriding & wheels) / linear earthworks
IRON AGE	early	390	hillforts / (widespread introduction of iron)
	middle	80	banjo enclosures / brochs
	late	0 BC/AD	raths / (first coins) / oppida

THE ROMAN PERIOD

(page 25) or Creswell Crags (page 75), but most settlements comprised temporary encampments, often beside a river or lake, as at the Barnfield Gravel Pit site, Swanscombe (page 52).

By the time of the last glacial advance, the Devensian, the Neanderthal population had in turn been succeeded by people who were genetically identical to us, *Homo sapiens sapiens*. During the height of the Devensian glaciation Britain was deserted, but after the retreat of the ice about 12,000BC, people returned. Hunting animals and gathering fruits and plants remained the mainstay of the economy, and communities still moved about a great deal in search of food. Toolmaking had changed again, and the late upper Palaeolithic traditions are usually known as Creswellian.

By about 10,000BC the landscape had changed from open tundra to a closed woodland dominated by pine and birch. The climate became warmer, and soils became richer. New tools and weapons were developed to hunt the animals of the forests, such as red deer, roe deer, wild boar and cattle, these

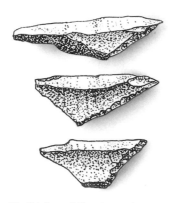

Mesolithic flints, probably used as spear tips

changes heralding the beginning of Mesolithic times.

Between about 8000BC and 6000BC rising sea levels severed the land bridge between Britain and the Continent. From then on, Britain developed its own traditions of hunter-gathering. The picture of life about 4500BC is one of a fairly numerous, but widely scattered population dependent mostly on red deer, wild cattle, wild boar, plants, and, along the coastline, marine resources.

NEOLITHIC FARMERS

Probably the single most significant event in the history of the British countryside took place between about 4400BC and 3800BC when farming was first adopted. This marks the beginning of the Neolithic period.

The idea of manipulating plants and animals to provide a more predictable food supply undoubtedly originated in the Near East. But whether it was adopted in Britain as a result of colonisation by farming communities or by native hunter-gatherer groups emulating their Continental neighbours is impossible to say.

Early farming communities had a considerable impact on the countryside, most notably by clearing woodland, introducing cereals (wheat and barley), and establishing grassland on which to graze cattle, pigs, and, to a lesser extent, sheep. Well-drained, easily cultivated land attracted most interest, especially major river valleys and downland in central and southern England. The uplands were only used for hunting and as sources of fine stone for the manufacture of tools and weapons (see Graig Lwyd, page 63, and Langdale, page 93).

Farming brought many changes in its wake. Settlements became more permanent. Farmsteads comprising perhaps one or two wooden houses were dotted about the countryside, and throughout southern and eastern England there were large enclosures known as causewayed camps. Some of these, like Crickley Hill (page 28), were defended settlements, others, like Windmill Hill (page 22), may have been seasonal camps or meeting places.

Burial monuments were also built by early farming groups. At first these were small stone structures such as the portal dolmens (see Trethevy, page 42) and simple passage graves (see Trefignath, page 66), but after about 3800BC most groups seem to have built very much larger monuments, now called long barrows, which contained collective burials deposited in wooden or stone chambers (such as West Kennett, page 22). Several regional traditions of long barrow construction can be distinguished, including the Cotswold-Severn type, earthen long barrow type and Clyde-Carlingford type. The Cotswold-Severn tradition, particularly

well represented in this book, involved tombs with trapezoidal mounds (the main characteristic) and chambers with front and side entrances (Belas Knap, page 25, and West Kennett are excellent examples). In all cases, however, the burial rites which took place at these different types of monument were complicated and drawn out. They involved not just funerals but also ceremonies at which bones from partly decomposed bodies were moved about within the different sections of the chamber and entrance passage.

A preoccupation with long monuments during the Neolithic is shown by the bank barrows (see Maiden Castle, page 31) and cursuses (see Rudston Area, pages 97—8).

Among the other changes associated with the adoption of farming were the introduction of pottery and the manufacture of a wide range of new tools and weapons. Mines for flint and stone were established (see Cissbury, page 47, and Grimes Graves, page 76) and trackways were built in wet areas such as the Somerset Levels (page 36) to facilitate communications (there were no wheeled vehicles at this time).

A seasonal gathering at Windmill Hill

LATE NEOLITHIC FARMERS

By 3000BC many parts of southern England which had previousy been densely occupied went into a period of decline. Long barrows were no longer built, causewayed camps were abandoned, and woodland grew back on land which had been cleared. New types of heavily decorated and rather crude pottery known as Peterborough ware became common.

A Neolithic tool kit — antler 'pick', ox shoulder blade 'shovel' and wickerwork basket

In the far west of Britain and Scotland the picture was rather different. Here the small settlements of earlier times grew in size (see Skara Brae, page 115). Long barrows of various sorts continued to be used, and a new range of round tombs developed. These new round tombs are highly regionalised and include developed passage graves in Anglesey (see Barclodiad y Gawres, page 56) and Orkney (see Maeshowe, page 114), entrance graves in West Penwith (page 33) and the Scilly Isles (see Bant's Cairn, page 24), and so-called Clava Cairns around Inverness (page 105).

The inspiration for the developed passage graves may have come from Ireland, a link which is strengthened by the presence of curvilinear designs, typical of the Boyne Valley in Ireland, on monuments in Anglesey and Orkney. Cremation burials replaced inhumations (burial of the unburnt corpse), and a new type of pottery known as grooved ware appeared. This ware, distinctive because of its decoration which imitates the weave of wicker baskets, became very popular, and by 2800BC was being used in all parts of the country.

Throughout Britain circular monuments began to replace the long structures of earlier periods, and from around 3000BC new ceremonial monuments such as henges (see Avebury Ring, page 23) and stone circles (see Castle Rigg, pages 90—1), together with novel burial monuments such as round barrows (see Priddy, page 35), ring cairns (see Brenig Valley, page 56) and enclosed cremation cemeteries (see Stonehenge, page 41) became common.

THE BRONZE AGE

The introduction of metalworking about 2500BC traditionally marks the start of the Bronze Age, but the new technology did little for the majority of the population as most of the early products were luxury items such as daggers, trinkets and ornaments. Single graves under round barrows were by this time common throughout Britain, and those of important people were richly furnished with fine objects including metalwork, beautifully made flintwork and heavily decorated pottery.

Grooved ware was succeeded by beaker pottery. Beaker pottery is distinctive because of its high quality, fine decoration and beautifully curved shapes; some beaker pots may even have been used as drinking vessels as the name suggests.

The climate of Britain between about 2000BC and 1500BC was warmer and drier than today. Upland areas such as Dartmoor, the North York Moors and the Cheviots were as intensively farmed as the lowlands. Much of the landscape was organised in a uniform way, with large, regular fields, paddocks and grazing areas. Farmsteads and enclosed settlements (see Grimspound, page 29) were common in most areas. In southern England there were also a few larger ditched enclosures of middle Bronze Age date, possibly tribal meeting places or trading centres (see Norton Fitzwarren, page 32).

Ceremonial monuments of the period include some types which carried through from earlier times — stone circles and henges, for example — as well as some new types including avenues (see West Kennett Avenue, page 23), stone rows (see The Nine Maidens, page 32) and standing stones (see The King Stone, Rollright, page 53).

Common to many Bronze Age ceremonial monuments is a concern for orientation and alignment. The focus of attention varied from one part of the country to another, but the rising and setting of the sun and moon seem to have interested many communities.

Burial rites changed during the course of the Bronze Age, from burial of complete corpses to a preference for cremations. Round barrows were used for the majority of burials, and barrow cemeteries developed (see Five Barrows, page 49). Beakers were replaced by new styles of pottery — food vessels and collared urns — which were used either as pots to accompany the dead or as vessels to hold cremated remains.

By about 1000BC many upland areas were in serious decline, fields and settlements were being abandoned and the population seems to have retreated to lower ground. Even in southern England arable cultivation declined, and

there is some evidence of the widespread adoption of cattle herding. The cause of these changes is not precisely known, but may have been connected with the onset of a colder and wetter climate.

Wet places seem to have attracted a great deal of attention from about 1000BC onwards, and much of the very fine metalwork made between this time and the Roman Conquest was deliberately deposited in rivers, lakes and bogs (see Llyn Cerrig Bach, page 67), perhaps as grave goods or as dedications to water gods.

There were social consequences too. Large communities were forced to live in smaller areas, there was greater competition for land, and considerable tension and unrest developed. New weapons of the period included swords and shields, and it was at this time that horse riding and wheeled vehicles first appeared on the scene.

THE IRON AGE

By 800BC hillforts were being built in the west of England, and within a century or so several thousand had been established across western, central and northern England, and in southern Scotland. Most were small, heavily defended sites.

At about the same time iron became widely used for tools and weapons, but this was probably not so much a technological revolution as a necessity in the face of difficulties in obtaining supplies of copper, tin and lead to make bronze. After the initial spate of hillfort construction, the picture of settlement and economy during the Iron Age was one of regional diversity, with a climate like that of today.

The Chysauster Iron Age settlement, Cornwall

In the west of England, Wales and northern Scotland, settlements were mostly defended farmsteads and small hamlets of various sorts. These include cliff castles in Wales and Cornwall (see The Rumps, page 36), courtyard houses in Cornwall (see Chysauster, page 34), enclosed farmsteads in north-west England (see Dod Law, page 92) and duns and brochs in Scotland (see Dun Carloway Broch and Dun Mor, both page 108).

In southern England, the Welsh Marches, parts of the Pennines and the Scottish borders, a simple hierarchy of settlement may be glimpsed. The early hillforts were replaced after about 400BC with much larger defended enclosures, the so-called developed hillforts (see Danebury, page 48). Around about the hillforts were smaller settlements represented by enclosures of different sorts and in some cases groups of unenclosed houses. Fields and grazing areas surrounded the hillforts and other settlements, individual land-holdings sometimes being demarcated by a system of linear earthworks.

In the Midlands, eastern England and East Anglia hillforts were rare, and here settlements included village-like groups of houses and enclosures representing farmsteads and hamlets. The landscape was well ordered with fields defined by hedges and ditches, trackways linking settlements, and unenclosed grazing areas beyond the more intensively used enclosed land.

Iron Age burials are generally rare. Rivers, lakes and wet places continued to be important, and perhaps used as burial places. The graves of a few male warriors and rich females have been found in central and southern England, but these represent the exception rather than the rule.

This pattern of regional diversity remained roughly constant until the Roman Conquest, except in south-east England. Here, some communities were strongly influenced by the affluence and high living of the Roman world, and tried to emulate Mediterranean customs. Coins came into use, again following Mediterranean practices, and large settlements known as *oppida* (see Wheathampstead, page 54, and Camulodunum, page 46) provided centres for trade and commerce in the years leading up to the Conquest.

USING THIS BOOK

Ancient monuments can be enjoyed in many different ways: as places of escape for peace and quiet, for recreation, for education, or as focal points on a walk, car tour or pony trek. Monuments provide inspiring and challenging subjects for painting, sketching, photography or writing. Imagination is the only constraint on what you can achieve.

When viewing a site try to visualise it as it might have been in prehistoric times. Capture in your mind's eye any ramparts or banks with vertical outer faces, and the dazzling brightness of bare earth, rock and upstanding stones before any lichen, grass or shrubs took hold of the site. Contemplate how many people occupied or visited the site you are looking at. Were they there all the time or did they only come for special occasions or in times of trouble? What was their mood? Did they live there, work there, retreat there out of fear, congregate there for ceremonies at special times? Or was it only at funerals and solemn occasions that our ancestors gathered there?

Think about how long it took to build the monuments you see with simple tools, and look carefully at the construction techniques which prehistoric people used. Visualise if you can the countryside around the sites you visit as it might have been in the past. Was it, for example, tundra, dense woodland, open grassland, fields or moorland? Above all, remember that no matter how isolated and remote a site may appear today, thousands of people will have been there before you, creating, using or admiring the monuments and landscapes that you see.

The ancient sites which are promoted as tourist attractions are usually signposted from main roads. Others can be more difficult to find and it is often useful to take with you a map showing footpaths (1:50,000 scale or larger). To help you pinpoint the position of the monuments mentioned in this guide on an Ordnance Survey map, a standard National Grid Reference (NGR) is given after each entry.

All ancient monuments are owned by somebody. Many of those listed here are in the guardianship of English Heritage, Cadw—Welsh Historic Monuments, the Scottish Development Department (Historic Buildings and Monuments), the National Trust, or a local authority, and are therefore open to the public. Others lie in public open spaces, or can be seen from a public right of way. At the time of going to press, all the monuments in this book were open, accessible, or easily visible to visitors. Arrangements are, however, constantly changing, and if you are ever in doubt about access always ask permission from the landowner: inclusion in this book does not imply any right of access.

Most prehistoric monuments can be visited at any reasonable time, but those under private management or in the charge of a custodian usually have restricted opening hours. Such sites are marked with an asterisk (*) in the text, and are listed on page 116. Suggestions for good museums to visit are also given — please see page 116. To avoid disappointment it is advisable to check opening times of sites and museums in advance if making a long journey.

Always observe the Country Code when visiting ancient sites, and never damage monuments by picking up stones, digging holes, lighting fires or taking bits away. The unauthorised use of a metal detector on an ancient monument is against the law.

Appropriate footware and clothing are always advisable. A torch is useful at barrows with accessible chambers; a candle is even better, because it gives a more authentic light!

Early Bronze Age artefacts — a beaker, stone battle axe, flint dagger and jet button — discovered at a barrow burial, Humberside

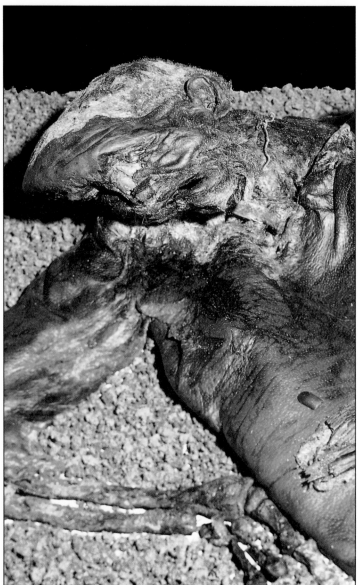

The remains of an ancient human body, known as Lindow Man, found in a bog at Lindow Moss near Wilmslow, Cheshire, in 1984. It seems that he was ritually slaughtered

Main picture: *Stones from the huge Avebury Ring*
Top right: *The West Kennett Long Barrow, one of the wealth of ancient sites in the Avebury area, Wiltshire*
Top left: *Inside the Neolithic tomb at West Kennett*

The huge Long Stone, Gloucestershire, is pierced by holes possibly caused by weathering

THE WEST COUNTRY

The Hurlers, Bodmin Moor

*N*o other part of Britain contains such a wealth of visible prehistoric monuments as England's West Country. Barrows of all shapes and sizes, hillforts, linear earthworks, henges and stone circles are especially numerous both in Wessex and on the Cotswolds. Such famous sites as Stonehenge and Avebury in Wiltshire, and Maiden Castle in Dorset, are located on the chalk downs in the south of the area. Further north in the limestone country of Gloucestershire lie the quaintly named Hetty Pegler's Tump and the Belas Knap long barrow.

In the Somerset Levels there are the remains of ancient wooden trackways leading from the dry islands out into the peat-covered fens, which date back to the times when wet marshes were extensively used for hunting, fishing and fowling. The rugged coastline of Devon and Cornwall hosts many sites distinctive of the West Country, including cliff castles and the settlements of small fishing communities.

The uplands of Mendip, Exmoor, Dartmoor and Bodmin Moor all contain abundant monuments from the Bronze Age, a time when the climate favoured dense occupation of the high ground where only bracken and gorse now flourish. Stone circles and stone rows are a distinctive feature of these areas. In the extreme south-west, on the heaths of West Penwith, land divisions and fields set out in later prehistoric times still form the framework of the countryside as it exists today.

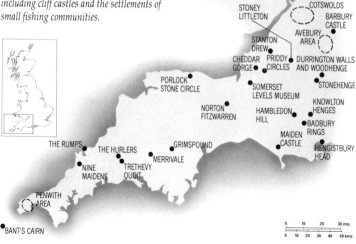

AVEBURY AREA,
near Marlborough, Wiltshire

Around the village of Avebury in the heart of the Marlborough Downs are some of the most astonishing and mysterious Neolithic and early Bronze Age monuments in England. What makes them unusual is their size, for although many prehistoric sites are large, those near Avebury almost look as though they were built by giants.

Many of the Avebury monuments have been excavated, and some of the finds are displayed in **Avebury Museum*** (see page 116).

The first site to visit, and also the earliest, is **Windmill Hill** *[NGR: SU 087714]*, about 1¼ miles north-west of Avebury village. Occupation began at Windmill Hill about 3800BC with a few houses in a woodland clearing, and it was shortly after, around 3700BC, that the causewayed camp, one of the largest in Britain, was built. This too was probably a settlement, although it may only have been occupied when the inhabitants of the surrounding downland came together for the purpose of seasonal festivals and gatherings.

Three roughly concentric lines of earthworks bounded the camp, and all of the inner ditch, part of the middle ditch, and a short length of the outer ditch can still be traced on the ground today. Broken pottery, flint tools, animal bones and a few infant burials have been found in the ditches. The four large and impressive Bronze Age round barrows on the hill were built long after the causewayed camp had been abandoned.

Of similar date to Windmill Hill causewayed camp is the massive **West Kennett Long Barrow** *[NGR: SU 104677]* which lies on a narrow windswept chalk ridge about 2½ miles to the south-east. This barrow measures over 100m long. At the eastern end is the chamber, which can still be entered. It is now roomy and bright inside, but when in use about 3800BC it would have been dark (the

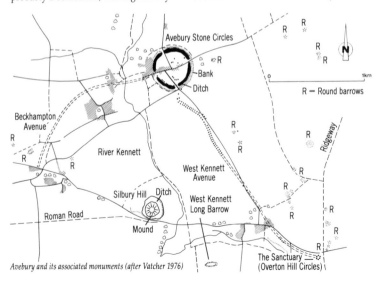

Avebury and its associated monuments (after Vatcher 1976)

glass skylights are modern!) and the floor strewn with rotting bodies and human bones.

About 3300BC the tomb fell out of use and was blocked up. Soil was dumped in the chambers, and the three enormous stones which still partly block the entrance were erected across the front of the mound.

Avebury Ring *[NGR: SU 103700]* was being built around the time that West Kennett was being blocked up. The great chalk bank of this enormous henge still stands over 5m high, and it is possible to walk round its entire circumference, a distance of nearly a mile. Standing on top of the bank looking into the centre gives the best view of the monument, for not only can you appreciate its scale, see all four entrances and look down on the flat central area, but also, immediately in front of you, gaze at the huge ditch nearly 25m wide and originally some 9m deep (about twice what it is today).

Around the inner lip of the ditch stands a ring of upright sarsen slabs. Originally there were 98 stones, many of very large size, the heaviest weighing over 40 tons. Two smaller stone circles, now incomplete, and a cove lie within the outer ring.

Snaking away from the southernmost of Avebury's four entrances towards Overton Hill some 1½ miles distant is the **West Kennett Avenue** *[NGR: SU 103697 to SU 118680]*. The stones of this avenue were deliberately chosen so that tall narrow ones alternated with squat diamond-shaped slabs, perhaps to symbolise male and female spirits.

At the far end of West Kennett Avenue, on Overton Hill, stands **The Sanctuary** *[NGR: SU 119680]*. Discovered

by aerial photography, this monument comprised a series of three successive round timber buildings, their main uprights now marked by concrete posts. About 2800BC, two stone circles were added (now also marked by concrete blocks). Six fine round barrows which date to between 1500BC and 2500BC are located on either side of the A4 next to The Sanctuary.

Mysterious Silbury Hill still refuses to reveal its secrets

The most enigmatic site in the Avebury area is **Silbury Hill** *[NGR: SU 100685]* which lies about 1¼ miles west of The Sanctuary, and is reputedly the largest prehistoric man-made mound in Europe. Although this great conical mound is known to contain some 350,000 cubic metres of chalk, and must of taken over 18 million man-hours to build, its purpose is quite obscure. No burial has ever been discovered within it. So much exploration has taken place that it is now unsafe to climb because of the danger of old tunnels collapsing.

Footpaths link Avebury, West Kennett and Silbury Hill, and there is good signposting and ample car parking.

BADBURY RINGS, *near Wimborne, Dorset. NGR: ST 964030*

This large and conspicuous Iron Age hillfort of about 7.2ha is very popular for Sunday walks. The defences, which run right round the hill, comprise two main ramparts and a third, less substantial, outer circuit. There are two original entranceways, one on the east and one on the west. The west entrance is unusual in having a rectangular projection from the middle rampart, and just inside it there is a slight depression in the ground which might be the site of a building. The east entrance is staggered to corner attackers.

Although never excavated, Badbury Rings was probably a major centre for communities living in this part of Dorset during Iron Age times. Later it lay at the junction of two main Roman roads, and a length of **Ackling Dyke** can still be seen as a low mound where it impinges on the outer rampart of the hillfort on the north-west side.

Three conspicuous mounds can be seen north of Ackling Dyke about $^{1}/_{3}$ mile west of the hillfort. These are Bronze Age round barrows.
NATIONAL TRUST

BANT'S CAIRN, *St Mary's, Scilly. NGR: SV 910124*

This fine late Neolithic entrance grave, now partly restored, is one of about 50 such tombs on the Scilly Isles and in West Penwith. It has a roughly circular cairn, about 12m in diameter, edged by two concentric walls. The outer wall possibly represents an enlargement of the initial structure. A rectangular chamber that can still be entered opens from the east side of the cairn. The chamber walls are slabs of local stone; notice the two large stones forming the entrance to the inner cairn. The roof, which now only survives over the inner part of the chamber, is formed by large capstones. Excavations in 1899 uncovered four piles of cremated bones within the chamber, together with a few pieces of pottery.

Nearby are the foundations of round and oval houses of a small Iron Age and Romano-British village. Other entrance graves which can be visited on St Mary's include **Innisidgen** *[NGR: SV 921127]* and **Porth Hellick Down** *[NGR: SV 929108].*
ENGLISH HERITAGE

Well-preserved Iron Age defences at Badbury Rings

BELAS KNAP, *near Winchcombe,*
Gloucestershire. NGR: SP 022254
Perhaps the most well known of all the
Neolithic long barrows constructed on
the Cotswolds, this site lies on a
windswept ridge above the town of
Winchcombe. Approaching the
monument from the north involves a
fairly steep climb along a footpath
(signposted) through grassy fields,
though the effort is well worth it.

Now fully restored, Belas Knap
displays many classic features of
barrows constructed in the Cotswold-
Severn tradition. The wedge-shaped
mound, now grassed over, measures
more than 50m long and stands nearly
4m high. At the north end is a deep
forecourt between two rounded horns,
and in the back of the forecourt is a false
portal resembling the H-shaped setting
at the front of a portal dolmen. The dry-
stone walling in the forecourt is partly
original Neolithic workmanship; only
the upper portions have been subject
to restoration.

Three chambers, all of which can
still be entered, open into the mound
from its long sides, while a fourth
chamber which lacks a roof opens from
the narrow southern end. Although
heavily restored, the three side chambers
still preserve the gloom and dampness
that must have pervaded them when in
use. The remains of about 30 people
were found in the burial chambers
during excavations which took place
early this century.

The name Belas Knap derives from
the Old English words *bel* meaning a
beacon and *cnaepp* meaning a hilltop. In
addition to Belas Knap itself, a small
round barrow is visible in the ploughed
field to the west of the site.

ENGLISH HERITAGE

CHEDDAR GORGE AND THE
MENDIP CAVES, *Somerset.*
Deep in the many steep-sided gorges
and combes that lie all around the
rugged Mendip uplands there are caves
and rock shelters that were occupied in
Palaeolithic and Mesolithic times. These
were the base camps for small
communities out hunting on the nearby
high ground.

In Cheddar Gorge is the impressive
Gough's Cave* (see page 116) *[NGR:*
ST 466539], fully geared up for the
modern visitor. This site was extensively
occupied in late upper Palaeolithic and
early Mesolithic times. Over 7,000
worked flints have been found,
including many tools and weapons. The
burial of an adult male, 'Cheddar Man',
was found in the cave, and is of early
Mesolithic date.

Other finds from the site include
decorated bone implements, incised
pebbles and a piece of amber. Many of
the finds from this site are displayed in a
small museum which is located in the
entrance to the cave.

To the east is another important
group of caves at **Wookey Hole*** (see
page 116) *[NGR: ST 533478]*. A cave
known as the Hyaena Den (south-east of
the great showcave) contained middle
Palaeolithic flint tools of Mousterian
tradition, overlain by deposits
containing upper Palaeolithic tools.

In Burrington Combe on the north
side of Mendip is **Aveline's Hole** *[NGR:*
ST 476586] which again contained late
upper Palaeolithic flint tools, harpoons
and human burials.

Caves such as these on Mendip
attracted attention in more recent times
too, and most reveal traces of occupation
in the later prehistoric, Roman and
medieval periods.

CENTRAL COTSWOLDS,
Gloucestershire

Near Uley, on the Cotswold escarpment overlooking the Severn Valley, is the Neolithic long barrow quaintly named **Hetty Pegler's Tump** [NGR: SO 789001], after Henry Pegler and his wife Hester who owned the site in the 17th century.

The narrow entrance and massive overlying stone slab at Hetty Pegler's Tump

Built in the Cotswold-Severn tradition, the mound is trapezoidal in plan, 36.5m long by 25.9m wide, and orientated roughly east to west. Two horns flank the narrow forecourt at the east end, and in the back of the forecourt is the entrance to the chamber. Reconstruction work in the late 19th century AD made the size of the entrance rather smaller than it was originally, and now the only way into the chamber is through a small wooden door at ground level (key available from the cottage at the top of Uley Hill just over ½ mile south of the barrow).

Once through the door, it is possible to stand up in the central passage. On the south are two side chambers, but two others on the north have been blocked up for safety reasons. Another chamber lies at the far end of the passage.

Of all the Cotswold-Severn tombs, this site alone retains something of its authentic atmosphere. Being inside the dark chamber with only a candle for light makes it easy to imagine what it must have been like at a ceremony or burial ritual here 6,000 years ago. But while in the chamber, notice also the roof construction, the use of dry-stone walling to fill the gaps between the orthostats forming the chamber walls, and consider the difficulties of moving human bodies about in the confined space. When excavated, this barrow contained the remains of at least 15 disarticulated skeletons.

About 1 mile to the north is **Nympsfield Long Barrow** [NGR: SO 794013], very similar to Hetty Pegler's Tump, but smaller and with only one pair of side chambers. The absence of capstones, which were removed long ago, allows an appreciation of the lay-out and design of the chambers. The remains of between 20 and 30 individuals were found here.

The roofless Nympsfield Long Barrow, devoid of its capstone and the mound which once covered it

About 1½ miles further north again is another long barrow: **The Toots,** *on Selsley Common [NGR: SO 827031].* This site has not been excavated, but is superficially similar in shape and size to Hetty Pegler's Tump.

The high density of Neolithic long barrows in the Cotswolds can be appreciated from the closeness of these three sites, and the fact that another dozen or more are known within 10 miles. The only other one in the area worth visiting is **Windmill Tump,** *Rodmarton [NGR: ST 933973].* This site shares many features with the barrows already described, but instead of a chamber opening from the back of the forecourt it has lateral chambers opening from the sides of the mound as at Belas Knap (page 25).

A fine late Neolithic round barrow known as **The Soldier's Grave** *[NGR: SO 794015]* can be visited at the same time as the Nympsfield Long Barrow. This barrow is 17m in diameter and in its centre (now marked by a deep hollow) a boat-shaped cist was discovered containing the remains of at least 28 individuals.

The Long Stone, *Minchinhampton [NGR: ST 884999],* is one of several standing stones on the Cotswolds which were probably markers for Bronze Age cemeteries. This example, of local limestone, is over 2.1m tall. It is said that when the stone hears the clock in the village strike midnight it dances around the field.

One of the most impressive Iron Age hillforts on the Cotswolds is **Uley Bury** *[NGR: ST 784989]* on the escarpment just over ½ mile south of Hetty Pegler's Tump. Enclosing about 13ha, the defences were constructed about 400BC and comprise two main

Uley Bury's overall defensive position is clearly visible from the air

lines of ramparts supplemented in places by a series of terraces and artificially steepened slopes. There are entrances at the north-east, south-east and south-west corners, all with in-turned ramparts and long entrance tunnels. Aerial photography has revealed abundant traces of occupation in the interior, but nothing of this is visible at ground level.

Parts of the Costwold uplands have remained relatively untouched by modern intensive agriculture, and accordingly preserve a wealth of archaeological sites of many different periods. Nowhere is this better demonstrated than on **Minchinhampton Common** *[NGR: SO 858010]* where it is possible to see, as grass-covered earthworks, a Neolithic long barrow known as **Whitefield's Tump,** a Bronze Age round barrow known as **Jacob's Knoll,** and two Iron Age enclosures known respectively as **The Bulwarks** and **Amberley Camp.**

CRICKLEY HILL, *near Cheltenham, Gloucestershire. NGR: SO 928161*

This promontory on the Cotswold escarpment with superb views up and down the Severn Valley has been intermittently occupied since about 4000BC. Excavations take place annually in the late summer, and a self-guided trail has been established, running between all main features at this fascinating site. The trail starts from the main car park (signposted).

The earliest monument on the hill was a causewayed enclosure with two concentric circuits of ditches probably constructed about 4000BC. After being remodelled several times it was completely rebuilt as a defended enclosure with just one line of defences (point 3 on the trail). Houses, roads and working areas suggest that in middle Neolithic times the site served as a defended village.

About 3200BC the enclosure was attacked, overrun and razed. Sometime later, perhaps during Bronze Age times, a bank barrow of earth over 90m in length was constructed on an east to west axis along the hilltop (corresponding with points 5/6).

In the 8th century BC a hillfort enclosing most of the promontory was constructed. The ramparts and elaborate entranceway of this fort can still be seen (points 1, 2 and 8). The first occupants of the hillfort lived in long houses, but following an attack on the site these were replaced by round houses. Coloured posts indicate the positions of the main uprights of these buildings. The site was again abandoned in the 3rd century BC. This marked the end of its life, for it was never subsequently reoccupied on a large scale.

Partly NATIONAL TRUST

DURRINGTON WALLS AND WOODHENGE, *Amesbury, Wiltshire. NGR: SU 150437*

Durrington Walls is a large, roughly circular enclosure, constructed about 2500BC. The site is best viewed from the car park to Woodhenge.

When new, Durrington Walls was of comparable proportions to Avebury Ring (page 23), but all that can be seen today are the denuded remains of the banks, and, when the fields are ploughed, a dark line around the inside of the bank indicating the position of the silted-up ditch.

However, much is known about the site as a result of excavations during the realignment of the A345 which runs through the enclosure. This work revealed that the ditch was 18m wide, 6m deep, and that the bank was originally about 27.5m wide and approximately 3m high.

Inside the enclosure were several massive circular timber buildings each over 30m in diameter. Finds included much grooved ware pottery, and the animal bones indicate that many pigs were consumed by the inhabitants or users of the site.

Woodhenge, immediately outside Durrington Walls to the south, is a small, classic henge monument, also of late Neolithic date. In contrast to its namesake Stonehenge (page 41), this monument contained a circular wooden building represented by six concentric circles of postholes (now marked by concrete pillars). The building is very similar to those found inside Durrington Walls, and one possibility is that Woodhenge was a shrine or temple adjacent to a settlement located inside the larger enclosure.

Partly ENGLISH HERITAGE

GRIMSPOUND, *Manaton, Devon.*
NGR: SX 701809

This site is probably the best-known middle Bronze Age enclosed settlement on Dartmoor. It lies in a shallow valley sheltered from the wind by hills to the north and south in an area of wild open moorland. When the site was occupied, between about 1600BC and 1200BC, the climate was warmer than today, and this part of Dartmoor was probably open grassland occasionally punctuated by small fields.

The Grimspound enclosure covers an area of about 1.6ha, and is bounded by a stout wall of granite boulders. The ancient entrance lies on the south side; the other gaps are modern. Inside are the foundations of over 20 buildings, all round in plan with walls up to 1m thick. Sixteen of them were probably dwellings and another eight possible storage buildings, barns or byres. The stone foundations visible today originally supported a wooden superstructure and a thatched roof.
ENGLISH HERITAGE

HAMBLEDON HILL, *near Blandford Forum, Dorset. NGR: ST 845126*

This hilltop overlooking the Vale of Blackmore to the west has a long and complicated history of occupation starting in middle Neolithic times when two causewayed camps and two long barrows were erected.

On the Stepleton spur was a small causewayed camp, possibly a settlement, although nothing remains to be seen of it. A bank and ditch ran north-west from this enclosure towards the main camp situated on the central knoll near the concrete trigonometry point. This enclosure, very difficult to see on the ground, was bounded by a single circuit of causewayed ditches, and may have been a ceremonial site in which bodies were exposed before being buried in long barrows. A small long barrow (now destroyed) lay immediately south of the main enclosure, while another, still visible as a grassy mound some 68.5m long, lies within the hillfort.

The most impressive and striking earthworks are those of the Iron Age hillfort, although the climb to them is steep. This fort, probably of several phases, covers 12.5ha and is bounded by two lines of ramparts. Its position makes it highly defensible against attack from almost any direction. There are three entrances, and inside numerous hut-platforms can be seen as flat scoops into the hillside.

About 1 mile south of Hambledon Hill is **Hod Hill** *[NGR: ST 856106],* another major Iron Age fortress.

HENGISTBURY HEAD, *Christchurch, Dorset. NGR: SZ 170907*

Throughout Iron Age times Hengistbury Head was an important port, and from about 150BC onwards became closely involved in international trade. Imports from the site included amphorae from the Mediterranean, glass, fine pottery and jewellery. The inhabitants minted coins, and were engaged in metalworking, shaleworking and glassworking. The fine natural harbour provided a safe anchorage for ships, and from about 700BC onwards the safety of the inhabitants of the peninsula was assured by means of a double rampart, much of it still visible.

Earlier than the Iron Age settlement are the 13 Bronze Age barrows which still survive in recognisable form. Eight, from the early Bronze Age, have been excavated.

THE HURLERS, *Minions, Cornwall.*
NGR: SX 258714

Once thought to be people turned to stone for playing ball on the Sabbath, this group of three stone circles was

The Hurlers, scattered across Bodmin Moor

actually an early Bronze Age ceremonial centre. Partly restored in 1936, the three circles lie in a roughly straight line on open moorland. The northern circle has 13 stones remaining, and is almost exactly circular. When excavated, the interior was found to be partly paved with granite slabs. The central circle, egg-shaped in outline, has 17 stones remaining. Near the centre is a recumbent stone. The southernmost circle has just nine stones remaining, and is again almost exactly circular.

Two upright stones known as The Pipers lie about 120m west-south-west of the central circle. Legend records that these represent the musicians playing for the hurlers when the group was turned to stone. The moorland around about is rich in prehistoric sites, including many barrows, enclosures, stone circles and a stone row.
ENGLISH HERITAGE

KNOWLTON HENGES, *Dorset.*
NGR: SU 025100

Although now dominated by the ruins of a Norman church, the ceremonial/religious significance of this site extends well back into prehistoric times when three late Neolithic henge monuments formed the focus of attention.

Only the central henge can easily be visited. It is oval in plan, with a long axis of about 107m, and entrances to the north-east and south-west. In places the grassy bank is still 3.6m high and the ditch 10.6m wide. The Norman church in the centre may have been built to Christianise what was perceived as an important pagan sanctuary.

The northern henge, invisible at ground level, is known from aerial photographs to be oval in plan. As with all henges, the ditch lies inside the bank. The southern henge, now partly covered by Knowlton Farm and the B3078, is circular in plan and about 244m across. Aerial photographs indicate entrances to the east and west.

East of the central circle is a very large round barrow, now covered in trees, about 41m in diameter and over 6m high. Near the northern circle is another circular enclosure, with a ditch

The central henge at Knowlton neatly encircles a ruined Norman church

outside its bank. Known as the Old Churchyard, this site may well be of relatively recent date.
Partly ENGLISH HERITAGE

MAIDEN CASTLE, *Dorchester, Dorset.*
NGR: SY 669884
This is certainly the finest hillfort in
southern England, made famous by Sir
Mortimer Wheeler who excavated here
between 1934 and 1936. The lofty
ramparts that now dominate the site
offer magnificent views over the Dorset
Ridgeway, and make for good walking.
The hilltop was used as the site for a
causewayed camp in middle Neolithic
times, but nothing of this is now visible.
Later in the Neolithic a bank barrow
over 545m long was built over the raised
remains of the causewayed camp, and
parts of this mound can still be seen.

The massive hillfort came next and
was constructed in three stages. First,
about 700BC, the eastern end of the hill
was enclosed by a single rampart. Next,
about 400BC, the fort was enlarged by
extending the rampart to encompass the
whole hill. Entrances were built at either
end. In the third phase, probably about
100BC, the defences were extended by
the addition of an outer bank and ditch,
and the elaboration of the entranceways.
This is how the site appears today.

Excavations inside the hillfort
revealed circular houses, roads, storage
pits and a shrine. The site was taken by
the Roman army in AD43 or AD44
during a savage battle. The body of one
of the defenders, shot in the back by a
ballista bolt (hurled from a catapult), can
be seen in Dorchester Museum. A
temple, the foundations of which can be
seen inside the fort, was constructed
during Roman times.
ENGLISH HERITAGE

MERRIVALE, *near Tavistock, Devon,*
NGR: SX 551746
This group of early and middle Bronze
Age ceremonial monuments, partly
restored, lies beside the B3357 on wild
open moorland. It is easily accessible
from the road, but the ground is rough
and sometimes boggy.

The focus of the site is a pair of
double stone rows. Notice that the
eastern ends of both rows are marked by
large triangular-shaped stones, and that
the southern row has a small cairn near
its centre, from where a single line of
upright stones extends south-westwards
for about 43m.

To the south are a stone circle, a
cairn, two standing stones and a large
burial cist that was robbed of its
contents many centuries ago. North of
the stone rows, on both sides of the
main road, are numerous Bronze Age
hut circles, possibly the foundations of
houses occupied by the users of the
nearby ritual monuments.
ENGLISH HERITAGE

Merrivale's stones march in a row across Dartmoor

NINE MAIDENS, *St Columb Major, Cornwall. NGR: SX 937676*

Romantically named, this line of nine upright stone slabs was constructed about 1700BC as a ceremonial site. It is a typical example of a stone row, although sadly only five of the stones remain more or less complete. Of the rest, one is fallen, two are just stumps, and one has been broken up and almost completely removed.

The purpose of this and other stone rows is not known with certainty. One possibility is that, like avenues, they were ceremonial ways — certainly, many rows are aligned on cairns, burial monuments or stone circles. But some, like the Nine Maidens, are not obviously associated with other monuments, and another idea is that they mark significant astronomical events. The trouble with this second theory is that few stone rows are straight, and there is

The enigmatic Nine Maidens

no common alignment among them to indicate which astronomical events were being marked.

NORTON FITZWARREN, *near Taunton, Somerset. NGR: ST 195263*

Set on a low hill overlooking the Vale of Taunton Deane, this Bronze Age enclosure and Iron Age hillfort is best seen by following the self-guided trail which starts at the car park in Blackdown View. Leaflets are available from County Hall in Taunton, but unfortunately not at the site itself.

The earliest occupation of the hilltop was probably during lower Palaeolithic times, but nothing of these activities, nor indeed the Neolithic

Norton Fitzwarren Archaeological Trail (after Somerset County Council 1985)

Ravine

Portion of Bronze Age bank surviving

N

Ravine

Hilly Park

Ravine

Key

---- *Paths*

⬯ *Bronze Age enclosure*

Iron Age defensive bank

Blackdown View

car park

settlement that also once existed on the hill, can be seen today. About 1300BC a rampart was constructed enclosing an area of 2ha. Part of this can be seen as a grassy mound on the eastern side of the hill at point 10 on the trail. Excavations show that the enclosure was an important meeting place for local communities and among the finds was a hoard of eight very finely made bronze bracelets and three axes.

Later, about 500BC, the hilltop was refortified. The ramparts of this Iron Age hillfort are still visible as substantial banks, and there is an entrance on the north-east side at point 8 on the trail. Like many hillforts in south-west England, Norton Fitzwarren continued to be occupied after the Roman Conquest of the area about AD50.

PENWITH AREA, *Cornwall*
Within this small area of picturesque moorland and enclosed pasture in the extreme south-west of Cornwall there are exciting traces of many prehistoric settlements, burial monuments and ceremonial sites. Indeed the whole landscape of West Penwith that we see today still shows the land divisions and enclosures that were used in prehistoric times.

Lanyon Quoit, possibly the best-known Neolithic burial chamber in Cornwall

Among the earliest sites in Penwith are the chambered tombs, in this area known as 'quoits'. **Lanyon Quoit,** *Madron [NGR: SW 430337]*, is probably one of the most dramatic and most photographed sites in Cornwall. But what we see today is in fact a reconstruction, dating back to 1824, of what was once a much larger chamber. Human bones have been found within the chamber, and traces of a long, low mound can just be seen round about, suggesting that the stone chamber was once part of a long barrow.

Less disturbed quoits can be seen at **Chun,** *near Morvah [NGR: SW 402339]*, which is set in a low round mound, **Mulfra** *[NGR: SW 452354]* and **Zennor** *[NGR: SW 469380]*.

Also possibly of Neolithic date is the **Men-an-Tol,** *Madron [NGR: SW 427349]*. This strange and unique monument now comprises three stones set in a straight line, the central stone being pierced by a round hole made by working from both sides. How much of the monument has been lost, and whether the stones remain in their original positions, is unclear. A person can crawl through the hole in the centre stone, and children apparently used to be passed through it as cure for rickets.

Of the later Neolithic period, the small entrance grave recently restored at **Bosiliack,** *Madron [NGR: SW 431342]* is worth visiting because of its similarities with the entrance graves of Scilly (page 24), although it is rather a long way from the nearest road and involves walking along some fairly rough footpaths. At **Carn Gluze** *[NGR: SW 355312]* the remains of a multi-period burial monument can be seen. The first phase of this site comprised a stone cairn revetted by two concentric walls, within the innermost of which were three stone cists. Two of the cists contained burial urns. Later, this structure was enclosed by a much larger cairn, and an entrance grave was constructed in the south-western part of the enlarged mound.

Stone circles of exceptional quality are abundant in West Penwith. **The Merry Maidens,** *St Buryan [NGR: SW 433245]*, otherwise known as the Stone Dance, is perhaps the most impressive and on a misty morning you can almost hear the prehistoric users of the site about their ceremonies. Two standing stones outside the circle to the north are called The Pipers, while the one to the west is The Fiddler. A legend common to many stone circles in the

West Country (see also page 30) records that 19 maidens and their musicians were turned to stone here for the sin of dancing on a Sunday.

The totally unspoilt **Boscawen-un** circle [NGR: SW 412273] has 19 upright stones around its circumference but here there is also a single stone in the centre. In AD1928 the Gorsedd of the Bards of Cornwall were inaugurated in the circle; modern bardic circles are used in much the same way in Wales.

Chysauster*, *near Gulval* (see page 116) [NGR: SW 472350] is an Iron Age settlement comprising a series of eight houses arranged in pairs along a street. Each house has an entrance facing east or north-east — away from the prevailing wind — thick outer walls, a courtyard immediately inside the entrance, and from three to six rooms opening from the courtyard. It is thought that animals were kept in the

courtyard. The village also contains a *fogou* which is a long, narrow underground chamber possibly used for storing food and as a hide-out in times of unrest.

Carn Euny, *Sancreed [NGR: SW 403288]* is similar to Chysauster in general layout, but has a larger and better preserved *fogou*. Excavations show that Carn Euny had a long history stretching from the 5th century BC through to the 4th century AD. During this time there were many changes to the structure and layout of the houses, and it must be remembered that not all the buildings were necessarily in use at any one time.

Also of Iron Age date is **Chun Castle** [NGR: SW 405339], a circular hillfort in a spectacular position defended by two concentric stone walls. There is a staggered entrance to the south-west. Parts of the gateway remain, including a pair of stone gateposts. The original dwellings were round, about 4.8m in diameter, and there may have been as many as 10 of them within the fort. The date of the well within the enclosure is not known.

Left: Looking from the hearth across the courtyard to the front entrance of a house at Chysauster
Below: Remains of the substantial foundations at Chysauster

PORLOCK STONE CIRCLE, *near Porlock, Somerset. NGR: SS 845447*
Ten standing stones and stumps together with 11 fallen stones are all that now remain of this once-impressive Bronze Age stone circle probably constructed about 2500BC. All the stones are local sandstone, undressed, and, in common with other circles on Exmoor, are fairly small in size, the largest being only 1m long. A small round barrow lies a few metres to the north-east.

Other stone circles on Exmoor include the **Withypool Stone Circle** *[NGR: SS 838343]* and **Almsworthy Stone Circle** *[NGR: SS 847416]*.

PRIDDY CIRCLES AND BARROW CEMETERY, *Wells, Somerset.*
NGR: ST 540527
This group of Bronze Age enclosures and barrows stands under pasture on the high windswept plateau of the Mendip Hills. The four Priddy Circles are circular enclosures, each about 183m in diameter and bounded by a small but neat bank and external ditch which can still be seen today. The circles are arranged in a straight line roughly north to south, the northernmost circle standing a little apart from the others.

At first sight they look like henges, but with ditches outside their banks they are clearly not in the mainstream of the henge tradition. Excavations in the southern circle revealed that the ditch here was U-shaped in cross section, 3.6m wide and 1m deep. The bank was revetted with timber uprights and faced with dry-stone walling. The true date and function of these circles have yet to be discovered.

East of the Circles are two groups of round barrows. **Priddy Nine Barrows**

The Priddy Circles' purpose is not known

[NGR: ST 538516] comprises a cluster of seven large and conspicuous barrows with two outliers to the north-east. All seem to have originally contained cremation burials.

Nearby is the **Ashen Hill Barrow Cemetery** *[NGR: ST 539514]*, which contains eight equally large barrows arranged in a row. All the barrows have been explored at some time, and have yielded a variety of burials including cremations in pits, urns and cists. The second barrow from the east appears to have been the most richly furnished as the cremated remains of an adult were accompanied by beads of amber and faience (a kind of glass), a bronze knife or dagger, and a small pottery vessel known as a grape cup. This was probably the burial of a local chief, perhaps someone who derived wealth from exploiting the rich sources of lead (used in making bronze) which can be found on the Mendips.

THE RUMPS, *St Minver, Cornwall.*
NGR: SW 934810
A magnificent late Iron Age cliff castle occupied between about 200BC and AD70, The Rumps is perched high on a rocky promontory jutting out into the Atlantic Ocean. It is a splendid place for a walk, and lies right beside the Cornwall North Coast Footpath.

Three lines of ramparts, not all necessarily contemporary, cut off the neck of the promontory and provide the main defences. Each rampart has a bank over 3.6m high, about 9m wide, and fronted by a ditch. Excavations revealed that the entranceway was defended by some kind of gatehouse.

Inside the castle the remains of several flat platforms can be seen; excavations show that timber-framed houses once stood on them. Finds included pottery, spindle whorls (used for spinning fleece into yarn), grindstones, querns (stone hand mills for grinding corn), thatch weights and various glass and metal ornaments. The inhabitants were seemingly fairly well-off since fragments of wine amphorae from the Mediterranean were found. The animal bones indicated that sheep were kept in large numbers, perhaps for their wool, together with lesser quantities of cattle and pig.

Other cliff castles in Cornwall worth visiting are: **Treryn Dinas,** *Treen* *[NGR: SW 397222]* and **Trevelgue Head** *[NGR: SW 827630].*
NATIONAL TRUST

SOMERSET LEVELS MUSEUM*,
Willows Garden Centre, near Westhay,
Somerset. NGR: ST 426414
Throughout prehistory the Somerset Levels were wet marshy areas exploited for their fishing, fowling, woodland and summer grazing. Wooden trackways were constructed to allow access, and because they became covered in peat shortly after their abandonment, and have never since dried out, many have been preserved.

The wood is very fragile after several thousand years in the ground and so it is not possible to display these prehistoric trackways where they were found. Some lengths have, however, been specially treated so that they can survive out of water, and these are displayed in Taunton Museum and in the British Museum.

In the Levels a small museum has been established at the Willows Garden Centre beside the minor road between Westhay and Shapwick. Here, pieces of preserved trackway and reconstructions of several tracks can be seen (and walked on). Among the reconstructions currently displayed is the Sweet Track which dates to about 3900BC and is recorded in the *Guinness Book of Records* as the oldest road in the world, and the Abbot's Way which is of early Bronze Age date.
WILLOWS GARDEN CENTRE

(see page 116)

General plan of The Rumps

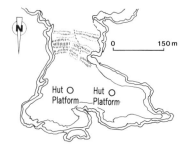

Bant's Cairn Neolithic tomb, on the Scilly Isles

Maiden Castle, Dorset, one of England's finest Iron Age hillforts, has complicated and ingenious defences

A Neolithic god figure discovered at the Somerset Levels

Inset: *The Sweet Track, reputedly the oldest road in the world, was constructed to allow access to the boggy Somerset Levels*

**PERIOD IIIb
After c.2000BC**

Selected bluestones erected in oval setting in centre of circle. Double circle of holes dug probably to hold remainder of bluestones, but this project was abandoned.

The site which, above all others, is synonymous with Britain's prehistory: the great temple at Stonehenge, Wiltshire

Butser Hill Experimental Iron Age Farm, Hampshire   Inset: *Trethevy Quoit, Cornwall*

STANTON DREW*, *Stanton Drew, Avon. NGR: ST 601634*

At the centre of this group of late Neolithic ceremonial monuments set in lush green meadows beside the River Chew is the Great Circle — a huge stone circle 112m in diameter. Two other circles can be seen nearby and a cove is located near the church.

ENGLISH HERITAGE (see page 116)

The setting of stones (the cove) beside the church at Stanton Drew

STONEHENGE*, *near Amesbury, Wiltshire. NGR: SU 122422*

Projecting skyward from the hallowed turf of Salisbury Plain like the gigantic wickets of some long-abandoned cricket match, the jumble of standing, leaning and fallen stones at Stonehenge probably represent the most famous, and certainly the most enigmatic, prehistoric monument in the whole of Europe. Nobody knows the full history or purpose of the site — perhaps that is what makes it so popular with visitors — but snippets can be pieced together.

Activity on the site began about 2800BC when a bank and external ditch were constructed to form a circular enclosure. Traces of this and its entrance can still be seen to the north-east. Cremation burials were placed in pits within the enclosure.

The site was then abandoned until about 2100BC when the enclosure was reused. A new axis aligned on the midsummer sunrise was adopted and a double circle of bluestones from south-west Wales was set up in the centre (see page 69). Parts of the avenue and the four station stones also belong to this period. The site was laid out to observe, and perhaps predict, the extreme risings and settings of the sun and moon, but the internal arrangements of the stones never stayed the same for any substantial length of time.

By about 2000BC the bluestones had been removed and an outer ring of 30 sarsen uprights linked by lintels, together with an inner ring of five trilithons (two upright stones with a third across the top), set up. This in turn was modified about 1600BC as the bluestones were reintroduced to form an oval setting within the outer circle. Pits were dug outside the outer circle. Finally, about 1500BC, the bluestones were again rearranged slightly, and the avenue lengthened to reach the River Avon at West Amesbury.

Why the main elements of this strange site were continually being changed around and modified is not known, neither is its precise function. Some would like to see it as a prehistoric computer, but like most of the other stone circles in use at the same time it probably had a much more simple role in regulating, and providing a focus for, ceremonies and rituals that its users considered important.

ENGLISH HERITAGE (see page 116)

STONEY LITTLETON, *Wellow, Avon.*
NGR: ST 735572
Approached across fields from the south
along a signposted path, this Neolithic
long barrow was constructed in the
Cotswold-Severn tradition about
3700BC. The cairn, edged by a neat dry-
stone wall, measures about 30.5m long
by 15.2m wide at the south-eastern end.
At the front are two projecting horns
flanking a forecourt, in the back of
which is the entrance to the chambers.
As you enter the chamber look for the
cast of an ammonite fossil on the left-
hand door jamb.

Stoney Littleton's entranceway

The burial chambers, which occupy
only a small proportion of the mound,
open from a central passage — three on
each side and an end-chamber. When
excavated, these chambers contained
confused heaps of bones representing
many individuals. Details of the burial
rites at other Cotswold-Severn barrows
suggest that corpses were first placed in
the entrance to the passage and that
later, as each body decomposed, it was
moved further into the passage until
ultimately, as dry bones, it was left to
rest in one of the side chambers.

The construction of the chamber
and passage is of interest, not only
because of the techniques used —
upright wall-stones carrying a partly

corbelled roof — but also because the
stones themselves were brought to the
site from outcrops over 5 miles away.
ENGLISH HERITAGE

TRETHEVY QUOIT, *Liskeard,*
Cornwall. NGR: SX 259688
Set on the edge of Bodmin Moor, this
Neolithic tomb is one of the largest and
most impressive in Cornwall. It stands
over 3m high and is constructed of
massive slabs of local stone. The
distinctive design, with six (originally
seven) upright slabs forming the walls of
the chamber and a single very large
sloping capstone forming the roof,
shows that it is part of the portal
dolmen tradition of tomb building found
throughout the west of England in early
Neolithic times.

Traces of an oval mound can still
be seen, but it probably never covered
the chamber. As with other portal
dolmens in Britain, access was not
through the front, which in this case is
closed by a very large slab, but rather
through a space above the side walls.
Today, the upright stone forming the
back of the chamber has collapsed
inwards, and a hole located in one
corner of the portal slab allows access
into the chamber.
ENGLISH HERITAGE

The tall Trethevy Quoit

SOUTH AND SOUTH-EAST ENGLAND

Cissbury, rich in prehistory

*A*lthough this part of England is densely populated there are still many prehistoric monuments to see, especially where agriculture has been less intensive in recent centuries. The chalklands of Berkshire, Hampshire, the Isle of Wight, Sussex and Kent are rich in Neolithic, Bronze Age and Iron Age monuments, as too are the Oxfordshire Cotswolds and the Chilterns. Among the more unusual kinds of site in the area are the massive late Iron Age enclosures, or oppida, of Essex and Hertfordshire. These were the nearest things to towns in prehistoric times, and the occupants frequently imitated Roman customs and high living.

The Thames Valley and London Basin were intensively exploited in prehistory, but while many sites have been recorded, especially through aerial photography, few survive as upstanding monuments worthy of a visit.

The south and south-east coast has always been an important area for trade and contact with the Continent, and this was certainly so in prehistoric times. In general, however, the coastline itself has been moving landwards over the past five or six thousand years, mainly through erosion, rising sea levels and sinking land levels. As a result some prehistoric monuments that are now on or near the coast were actually some distance inland when they were in use. Conversely, sites which once lay on the coast are in some cases now under the sea.

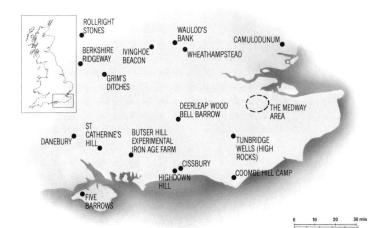

BERKSHIRE RIDGEWAY, *Oxfordshire*

This section of The Ridgeway runs towards Uffington Castle from Wayland's Smithy

Winding its way along the northern edge of the rolling Berkshire Downs from Streatley in the east to West Kennett in the west is an ancient track known as **The Ridgeway,** part of the great Icknield Way that ran from near King's Lynn in East Anglia to Salisbury Plain in Wiltshire.

Exactly when The Ridgeway came into being is not known, but because it passes so many prehistoric sites it was almost certainly used in pre-Roman times, and may even be of Neolithic or Bronze Age origin. Whatever its origins, The Ridgeway provides many pleasant walks and a variety of sites to visit along the way. One especially good stretch is near Uffington where, on fine days, there are superb panoramic views over the upper Thames Valley and the Vale of the White Horse. The sites described below can all be seen in the course of a short circular walk of about 3 miles from the car park at Uffington Castle [NGR: SU 297864]. In wet weather it is advisable to wear wellington boots for this walk because the route can get muddy in places.

The first site to visit is the wondrous **Uffington White Horse** [NGR: SU 302866], a few hundred metres north-east of the car park. This is probably the best known and most ancient of the numerous hill-figures in southern England, and was made by simply cutting away the turf and topsoil to reveal the white chalk bedrock beneath. The horse is highly stylised, with a single line forming the neck, body and tail, and an almost detached, bird-like head. Two of the legs are joined to the body, the others are detached. The best place from which to view the whole animal is to the north on the B4508 between Longcot and Fernham.

Similar horses are depicted on late Iron Age coins, and because of this it is generally accepted that the Uffington Horse is also of this date, perhaps a tribal emblem of the people who lived in the area during the Roman Conquest.

The Uffington Horse has to be regularly cleaned to keep it white. Up until the early years of this century, cleaning the horse seems to have been a two-day festival held every seven years.

Each festival, or pastime, attracted people from all the surrounding villages and involved games, races and dancing. Today, this merriment has ceased and the horse is cleaned by the workmen from English Heritage who now look after the site.

The flat-topped hill below the horse is known as **Dragon Hill.** It is not an archaeological site as such but, according to legend, was the place where St George slew the dragon.

About 200m south-west of the White Horse is **Uffington Castle** [NGR: SU 299864]. This Iron Age hillfort was probably occupied by the people who first made the White Horse. The ramparts are now grassy banks, but excavations in 1850 revealed that originally they were revetted by some kind of timber framing, and that the outside was faced with sarsen stones. There is a single entrance facing north-west, but look out for the way the bank turns outwards at this point to form a narrow entrance passage.

The Uffington White Horse, galloping in the direction of Uffington Castle

Leaving Uffington Castle join The Ridgeway leading westwards. The wide track that we see here today was created fairly recently — in the 18th century — when low banks were erected on either side to preserve the right of way from encroachment by ploughing; the breadth was fixed at 1 chain (20.11m).

About 1¼ miles along The Ridgeway is **Wayland's Smithy Long Barrow,** now restored and nestling peacefully in a clump of trees [NGR: SU 281854]. Excavated in 1962—3, this Neolithic long barrow proved to be of two phases. The earliest monument, not now visible, was a small oval mound covering a wooden mortuary house which contained the bodies of 14 people.

Wayland's Smithy, an impressive Neolithic construction

About 3500BC this simple structure was enlarged to what we see today. A monumental mound, some 55m long and edged with sarsen slabs, was built over the earlier structure, the material for its construction being quarried from flanking ditches (now filled in). Six great sarsen slabs which average over 3m high were set across the front of the mound to provide an impressive façade. At the same time, a cruciform chamber was constructed at the wider, higher end of the mound. This can still be entered, and when excavated was found to contain the remains of at least eight people, including a child.

Legend holds that an invisible smith lived at the site and that a horse left there with a penny would be well shod by the time the owner returned to collect it.

Return to the Uffington Castle car park via The Ridgeway.

BUTSER HILL EXPERIMENTAL IRON AGE FARM*, *near Petersfield, Hampshire. NGR: SU 7918*

Set within the Queen Elizabeth Country Park amid the chalk downs of Hampshire, the experimental Iron Age Farm on Butser Hill provides a vivid and moving impression of what life was like in Iron Age times.

The Iron Age comes to life at Butser Hill

The focus of the site is a full-size reconstruction of an Iron Age farmstead, based on excavated examples. Within an enclosure is a large round house built in 1976. Over 200 trees were used in its reconstruction, and the great conical thatched roof, its apex over 8m above ground, weighs 10 tons when dry. The building contains replica Iron Age household and farming equipment, and around about there are animal pens, pits and ovens.

The site is not just a static reconstruction. It is run as a working farm. Outside the enclosure there are fields and paddocks laid out as they might have been during the Iron Age, and stocked with authentic species of plants and animals. Ploughing, sowing and harvesting take place here, and throughout the season all sorts of experiments ranging from the making of pottery through to spinning and weaving using replica Iron Age equipment will be in progress.

The site is open afternoons Easter to end of September (see page 116)

(see page 116)

CAMULODUNUM *(Colchester), Essex. NGR: TL 963240*

The Trinovantes, the Iron Age tribe living in Essex before the Roman Conquest, had their capital (Camulodunum) in the area of modern Colchester. Much of the settlement lies under housing estates and factories, but traces of the former defences can still be seen in places.

The site lay on a promontory of some 31 square km (12 square miles) defined on the north and east by the River Colne, on the south by the Roman River, and on the west by massive dykes. Sections of these dykes remain at **Grymes' Dyke** *[NGR: TL 960247 to TL 962233 and TL 959230 to TL 956220]*; **Triple Dyke** *[NGR: TL 965246]*; and **Lexden Dyke** *[NGR: TL 976264 to TL 975258 and TL 973251 to TL 974246]*. Except for Triple Dyke, each comprises a single bank and ditch.

The inhabitants of Camulodunum emulated Roman customs, and were involved in trade with the Roman world. The **Lexden Tumulus** *[NGR: TL 975247]* contained the burial of one of their leaders, possibly King Addedomaros. Accompanying the cremation were many ritually broken objects including fine tableware, wine amphorae and jewellery. Following the Roman Conquest, Camulodunum became an important *colonia* for retired Roman army veterans. *Partly ENGLISH HERITAGE*

CISSBURY, *near Worthing, West Sussex.*
NGR: TQ 139080
On the western end of this commanding little hill overlooking Worthing are more than 200 hollows representing the partly filled shafts of Neolithic flint mines dating to about 3600BC. Unfortunately

berm some 3m wide, a deep ditch and a small counterscarp bank, was probably first constructed about 400BC. There are two entrances, one of which faces east, the other south.

During Roman times the hillfort was in decay, and the interior was

Cissbury's Iron Age banks enclose Neolithic flint mines

it is not possible to go down into any of the shafts, but excavations have revealed that some are up to 12.1m deep. When the miners reached good bands of flint they cut a series of radiating galleries out from the shaft to follow the seam. All the work was done with antler picks, levers and bone shovels. Baskets were presumably used to transport material up to the surface. Stone lamps which used a wick to burn fat provided light for the miners working underground.

When one shaft was exhausted another was dug nearby, the spoil being used to backfill the previous hole. Burials were sometimes inserted into the backfill, although in at least one case the body may be there because of an accidental fall.

Overlying the flint mines, and extending across much of the hilltop, is a roughly oval-shaped Iron Age hillfort of about 20ha. The single rampart, comprising a massive inner bank, a

cultivated. Later, at the end of the Roman period, the site was refortified by adding a turf capping to the bank. Some of the small enclosures within the fort may also date from this period.
NATIONAL TRUST

COOMBE HILL CAMP, *near Eastbourne, East Sussex. NGR: TQ 574021*
This Neolithic causewayed camp, now partly under picturesque woodland, has two roughly concentric circuits of ditches. It is oval in plan, but incomplete on the north side because of the steepness of the slope. Excavations in the 1930s uncovered large quantities of pottery, flint tools, arrowheads and quernstones (for grinding corn) in the ditches. A radiocarbon date from material in the ditch suggests that this causewayed camp was occupied around approximately 3200BC.

To the east of the camp are several round barrows [NGR: TQ 576023], one of which contained four splendid bronze axes, all of them broken.

DANEBURY, *near Stockbridge, Hampshire. NGR: SU 323377*

Shrouded by a canopy of mature beech trees, the hillfort at Danebury is set on a low hill overlooking a sea of arable land.

platforms for defenders using slings, a command post, and a narrow entrance tunnel in which invaders could be trapped. Exactly who the expected attackers were is not known, but they

Danebury's defences are explained with the help of an easy-to-follow self-guided trail

The site has been the subject of intensive study through excavation and survey, and has provided a completely new picture of the way Iron Age societies worked. A self-guided trail has been established to help visitors enjoy the site more fully. Danebury is within a country park, so there is ample parking and plenty of picnic and play areas.

In early prehistoric times Danebury was variously used as a burial ground and ceremonial site. Construction of the hillfort, which began in the 6th century BC, completely changed the character of the hilltop. A single timber-laced rampart was built all round the hill enclosing about 5.3ha. Later this was elaborated and extended so that by the 2nd century BC there were up to three lines of ramparts. The strength of these ramparts, which would originally have been about 2m higher than they are today, can be appreciated from point 9 on the trail.

The gateways were also strengthened when the ramparts were extended. Particularly impressive is the eastern entrance (points 2—4) with its elaborate system of outworks to provide

might have been neighbouring communities out to steal cattle or food.

Inside, the fort was laid out in an orderly fashion with a road running across the middle, circular houses set against the back of the rampart, and storage pits and granaries in the middle. A shrine may have occupied the very centre of the site. Over 200 people probably lived permanently in the hillfort at any one time, among them carpenters, metalworkers, potters, farmers and possibly also the overlords of the numerous farms and hamlets around about.

DEERLEAP WOOD ROUND BARROW, *near Dorking, Surrey. NGR: TQ 118481*

This very fine Bronze Age round barrow is preserved within a quiet and tranquil wood not far from the busy A25. The mound measures about 30.5m across, and you can clearly see its surrounding ditch and a low outer bank. No burial has been found under the mound, probably because the acid soil has completely dissolved it.

FIVE BARROWS, *near Shalcombe, Isle of Wight. NGR: SZ 390852*

This Bronze Age cemetery of eight round barrows irregularly arranged in a line running east to west lies along the top of a chalk ridge overlooking the south-west coast of the island.

The westernmost barrow is a bell barrow some 2.5m high, while the easternmost barrow is a disc barrow about 35.3m in diameter. The remaining six barrows are all bowl barrows and range in height from 0.5m to 2m. The tallest bowl barrow has a causeway across its ditch. Hollows in the tops of all the barrows in this cemetery suggest that they have been excavated in the past, but no records survive to indicate what was found.

Preparing tools and weapons to accompany a Bronze Age burial at a round barrow about 1700BC

Other barrow cemeteries on the Isle of Wight include: **Afton Down** [NGR: SZ 352857]; **Michael Moorey's Hump** [NGR: SZ 536874]; and **Shalcombe Down** [NGR: SZ 391855].

Like other such cemeteries in southern England, these monuments probably developed over a long period of time, perhaps four or five centuries. Whether the barrows were grouped together because the site was held to be sacred or because they were an obstacle to agriculture and so constructed along the edge of cultivated land is not known.

NATIONAL TRUST

GRIM'S DITCHES, *Berkshire/Oxfordshire.*

The rolling Berkshire Downs south-east of Wantage preserve some very fine stretches of linear earthwork, many of which are known as Grim's Ditch.

One particularly good section comprising bank and ditch follows the present Berkshire/Oxfordshire county boundary south-west of **Chilton** [NGR: SU 495839 to SU 418842]. It runs along the edge of the Downs, not in a straight line but twisting and turning, sometimes with very sharp corners. A number of Bronze Age barrows and field-banks lie on or very near the earthwork. Another well-preserved section of bank and ditch may be seen near **Aldworth** [NGR: SU 546785 to SU 570792].

Investigations of these meandering earthworks, sometimes called 'ranch boundaries', show that they are of late Bronze Age or Iron Age date and relate to a time when large tracts of downland in southern England were parcelled up for agriculture or pasture. Why this should have been necessary is not clear, but it may have been connected with factors such as a rising population, a worsening climate and greater concern about land ownership.

HIGHDOWN HILL, *near Worthing, West Sussex. NGR: TQ 093043*
An excellent place for picnics and leisurely walks, this imposing little hill overlooking Worthing and the narrow coastal plain has repeatedly attracted attention as a place for settlement. A farmstead stood on the hill in late Bronze Age times, and a hoard of tools and weapons found nearby were perhaps hidden by the occupants of this farm during a period of unrest. Nothing, however, now remains to be seen of this occupation; the earliest visible features are the grass-covered ramparts of a small Iron Age hillfort.

Highdown Hill has a long history of occupation

Excavations in 1939 revealed that the hillfort ditch was steep sided, about 2m deep, and separated from the bank by a narrow berm. The rampart was of chalk rubble secured by timber posts front and back. Little is known about occupation within the fort during Iron Age times, but the site was certainly reoccupied in the late 3rd and 4th centuries AD, and in the Saxon period a cemetery was established inside the ramparts of the fort.
NATIONAL TRUST

IVINGHOE BEACON, *near Tring, Buckinghamshire. NGR: SP 960169*
This small Iron Age hillfort of about 2.2ha occupies a prominent spur of Chilterns and is best approached by footpath from the south. Although set in a highly defensible position with extensive views to the north and west, the hillfort was probably only used for a short time in the 6th or 7th century BC, and it is likely that the defences were never completed.

Although heavily eroded, it is still possible to make out the ditch of the defences on the north and east sides, which survives as a level platform. A double platform representing the remains of the ramparts can be seen on the west side. The entrance was in the east corner. Excavations between 1963 and 1965 demonstrated that the ramparts were composed of chalk rubble with timber revetments front and back, as is common in early Iron Age hillforts.

Inside the fort were traces of round houses, one over 7.3m in diameter, structures which may have been granaries supported on four upright posts, and the postholes of a rectangular

Ivinghoe Beacon crowns the 230m Beacon Hill

wooden building. The pottery recovered during the excavations suggests that this site must have been among the earliest hillforts to be built in the area.
NATIONAL TRUST

MEDWAY AREA, *Kent*

The delightful Medway Valley and the area around about remains one of the least spoilt parts of north Kent and contains an interesting assortment of prehistoric monuments, of which the most spectacular are the well-known Neolithic long barrows. Ten of these tombs have been identified, of which five can easily be visited in the course of a leisurely day out in the area.

Starting west of the River Medway the first site to see is the **Coldrum Long Barrow** *[NGR: TQ 654607]*, probably the best preserved of all the Medway sites. It sits on a low ridge in the shadow of the North Downs and faces east towards the Medway. The mound is slightly wedge shaped, about 20m long, and edged with a ring of rounded sarsen boulders known as a peristalith. The chamber at the east end, partly restored, survives as four upright stones forming three sides of a simple box-like structure. Excavations revealed that at least 20 individuals had been buried in it. As visible today, however, the east end of the site has been truncated; originally the ground would have sloped away from the tomb more gently than it does now.

Just over a mile south of Coldrum are a pair of long barrows at Addington. The larger of the two, the **Addington Long Barrow** *[NGR: TQ 654592]*, lies west of the village and is crossed by the minor road leading to Wrotham Heath. The mound is 60.3m long by 14m wide. Traces of a peristalith and the remains of a collapsed chamber at the eastern end can still be seen.

About 100m north-west of the Addington Long Barrow is the **Chestnuts Long Barrow*** *[NGR: TQ 652592]*, accessible by asking

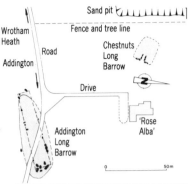

Top: Plan of the Chestnuts and Addington Long Barrows (after Philp and Dutto 1985)

permission at the house in whose grounds it stands (see page 116). Like Coldrum, the mound is slightly wedge shaped, originally about 20m long by 15m wide although much of it has now disappeared. The eastern end has an imposing façade of four large upright stones rather like Wayland's Smithy (page 45). The chamber opens from the middle of the façade and, like the other barrows in the Medway group, is a simple rectangular structure. A possible capstone lies to one side. Excavations in 1957 revealed the cremated remains of at least nine individuals, together with objects of late Neolithic date. It is likely, however, that the monument was constructed rather earlier than this period, at some time between 3800BC and 3000BC.

East of the Medway, the most impressive tomb is the curiously named **Kits Coty** [NGR: TQ 745608], best approached from the south along a narrow — and in places quite steep — path shaded by trees on either side.

Kits Coty, the burial tomb that has reputedly also served as a tiny dwelling

Apparently, the name Kits Coty was given to the site by a shepherd who used to live in the stone chamber, the word 'coty' meaning a tiny house.

Old pictures of the site show that originally the chamber which is visible today stood at the east end of a long mound that has now largely disappeared. At the west end of this mound there was once a large stone known as the General's Tombstone, but this was blown to bits in 1867 because it hampered cultivation of the field. The remaining chamber has three large uprights supporting a single massive capstone. There are no records of burials being found at the site.

About 500m south of Kits Coty, right beside the road to Aylesford, are the remains of another tomb known as **Little Kits Coty** [NGR: TQ 745604] or **The Countless Stones.** This jumbled group of stones represents the collapsed chamber and façade of a tomb rather similiar to the long barrows of Coldrum and The Chestnuts.

No settlements of Neolithic date are visible in the Medway area, but occupation sites of both earlier and later dates can be seen. At **Oldbury Rock Shelter** [NGR: TQ 585562], a number of flint handaxes of Mousterian type have been found, suggesting that middle Palaeolithic hunter-gatherer communities used the overhangs in the rock face as shelters. The importance of the area in Palaeolithic times is emphasised by the fact that only 12 miles north of this site is the **Barnfield Gravel Pit,** *Swanscombe* [NGR: TQ 598746], now a nature reserve, where numerous Acheulian flint tools and the bones of Swanscombe Man (who probably lived during middle Palaeolithic times) were discovered in the 1930s.

Oldbury Camp [NGR: TQ 582562] is a very large Iron Age fort of some 49ha, mostly bounded by a single rampart which follows the edge of a steep-sided plateau. It is generally well preserved but wooded. Excavations have revealed that although the site was originally of fairly simple construction with a bank of dumped rock and soil derived from the ditch, it was greatly strengthened just before the Roman Conquest, presumably to resist the invading army. The site was never very intensively occupied and may have been a place of refuge at times of unrest.

Entering Oldbury Camp by its south gate

ROLLRIGHT STONES,

near Chipping Norton, Oxfordshire.
Centred on NGR: SP 296308

A legend associated with the monuments visible at this site records that a witch turned a king, his knights and his men into stone.

The **Whispering Knights** is, in fact, the remains of a portal dolmen-type burial chamber dating to about 4100BC. Four stones still stand upright, while a fifth, probably the capstone, lies fallen. No mound is now visible, but one may well have existed here, as at Trethevy (page 42).

The **King's Men** is a very fine stone circle, about 31.6m in diameter, and dating to between about 3000BC and 2500BC. In 1882 the circle was restored by the addition of new stones to replace some which had been lost or removed. This may have given rise to another legend about the site which records that if you count the stones you never get the same number twice.

The Whispering Knights, Rollright Stones

The **King Stone**, once thought to be the remains of a Neolithic long barrow, is now known to have been the marker-stone for a cemetery dating to the early Bronze Age. Several small cairns containing cremations were discovered around the stone during excavations in 1979.

ST CATHERINE'S HILL, *near*

Winchester, Hampshire. NGR: SU 484276

Situated on a rounded chalk knoll towering over the River Itchen and with fine views over the historic town of Winchester, this hillfort of about 9ha was defended by a single rampart comprising a bank, an external ditch and a small counterscarp bank.

The only entrance lies on the north-east side. Excavations here in 1927—8 revealed that, when first constructed, the gateway was provided with a pair of guard chambers, one either side of the entrance passage. These were later demolished and the walls of the entrance passage faced with chalk blocks.

Altogether, this hillfort underwent at least four major phases of rebuilding, but in the later part of the Iron Age it was attacked, overrun and burnt, probably by the occupants of a neighbouring hillfort. Within the fort are the remains of a medieval chapel and an 18th-century AD turf-cut maze.

TUNBRIDGE WELLS, HIGH ROCKS*, *East Sussex/Kent border.*
NGR: TQ 561382
Perched above precipitous rock cliffs overlooking a narrow river valley is a fine Iron Age hillfort of about 8ha. The site is opposite the High Rocks Hotel (see page 116) and is approached up a

High Rocks is aptly named

steep footpath. The cliffs provide protection on the north-west side, but double ramparts define the remainder of the circuit and at the east entrance the ramparts are trebled.

Excavations have revealed two main phases of occupation, the first dating to about 100BC, the second towards the middle of the 1st century BC. The inner rampart with a stone-faced bank was built during the second phase, and the entrance strengthened. Mesolithic and Neolithic occupation has been found below the hillfort against the steep rock faces where overhangs provided rock-shelters.

WAULOD'S BANK, *Luton, Bedfordshire. NGR: TL 062246*
Now standing in a public park on the north-west edge of Luton, this site is one of very few late Neolithic enclosures known in eastern England. A grassy bank, still standing about 2m high in

places, forms the north, east and south sides of the enclosure, while the River Lea, which rises within the site, defines the west side. Pieces of late Neolithic grooved ware style pottery and many flint arrowheads have been found here. The site may have been a ceremonial focus connected with the source of the River Lea.

WHEATHAMPSTEAD, *Hertfordshire. NGR: TL 184135*
During the reign of King Cassivellaunus (died 40—35BC) the tribal focus of the Catuvellauni who occupied the Hertfordshire area may have been at Wheathampstead to the north-east of St Albans. Here, on a piece of raised ground in the valley of the River Lea, are the remains of a small *oppidum* of 35—40ha enclosed by two earthworks which are known locally as the **Devil's Dyke** and **The Slad.**

Map of the oppidum *and earthworks at Wheathampstead (after Saunders 1982)*

Excavations by Sir Mortimer Wheeler in 1932 revealed the extraordinarily large proportions of these earthworks: at its maximum, the ditch of the Devil's Dyke is 39.6m from lip to lip and 12.1m deep. This *oppidum* may have been the site where, according to the narrative in his book *Gallic Wars*, Julius Caesar defeated the Catuvellaunian forces in 54BC.

WALES

*T*he rugged and diverse landscape of Wales has always determined the distribution of settlement and agriculture. At times of favourable climate — during the Bronze Age for example — people lived and worked on the higher ground. But for most of prehistory the coastal fringe, the main river valleys and the lowlands were the focus of activity, and it is here that most of the best monuments are to be found.

The southern coast, in Glamorgan and Dyfed, was an important area for early and middle Neolithic settlement, as shown by the numerous long barrows. Throughout Wales there are Bronze Age stone circles, in some cases associated with stone rows in a way that is rather rare elsewhere.

North Wales, particularly Anglesey, was closely connected by trade and perhaps also kinship with Ireland. Special features of this area include the massive developed passage graves under great domed mounds and the hillforts or hilltowns set high on rocky mountain tops. The mineral wealth of central and northern Wales ensured that contacts with southern England were maintained from Bronze Age times onwards.

Wales was never as heavily Romanised as most other parts of southern Britain, and in the far west of the country prehistory really continued down into the 1st millennium AD.

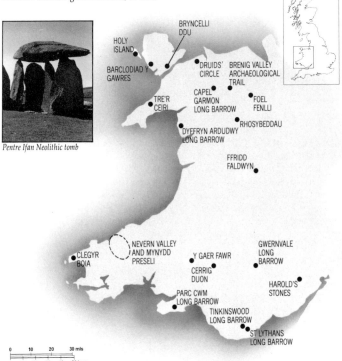

Pentre Ifan Neolithic tomb

BRYNCELLI DDU

HOLY ISLAND

BARCLODIAD Y GAWRES

DRUIDS' CIRCLE

BRENIG VALLEY ARCHAEOLOGICAL TRAIL

TRE'R CEIRI

CAPEL GARMON LONG BARROW

FOEL FENLLI

DYFFRYN ARDUDWY LONG BARROW

RHOSYBEDDAU

FFRIDD FALDWYN

CLEGYR BOIA

NEVERN VALLEY AND MYNYDD PRESELI

Y GAER FAWR

GWERNVALE LONG BARROW

CERRIG DUON

HAROLD'S STONES

PARC CWM LONG BARROW

TINKINSWOOD LONG BARROW

ST LYTHANS LONG BARROW

0   10   20   30 mls
0 10 20 30 40 50 kms

BARCLODIAD Y GAWRES,

near Rhosneigr, Anglesey, Gwynedd.
NGR: SH 328708

Set on the coast of Anglesey overlooking the Irish Sea, this developed passage grave of late Neolithic date is one of the finest tombs in Wales. Recently restored, the domed mound stands over 3m high and is visible from some distance away. Excavations revealed that it was built of turf with only an outer layer of stone.

A long narrow passage leads into the mound from the north-west and gives access to the chamber. Visitors wishing to enter the chamber can collect a key from the Wayside Cafe in Llanfaelog. The walls of both passage and chamber are formed of upright stone slabs but while the roof of the passage simply comprised stone slabs, the chamber was roofed with a corbelled dome. Five of the wall-stones are decorated with spirals, zigzags and wavy lines in a manner common in Ireland but very rare in Britain. The designs were made by lightly pecking the surface of the stones with a hard stone chisel.

Excavations in 1952—3 revealed cremation burials in the side chambers. Grave goods found in the tomb included a long bone pin. The site's expressive Welsh name translates as 'the Giantess's apronful', a reference to a widespread legend that monuments such as this were created by mythical giants dropping piles of stones on to the land inhabited by mortals.
CADW—WELSH HISTORIC MONUMENTS

BRENIG VALLEY ARCHAEOLOGICAL TRAIL, *near*
Cerrigydrudion, Clwyd. Starting in the car park at NGR: SH 984575

During the construction of the Brenig Reservoir high in the mountains of Clwyd during the early 1970s, some 50 archaeological sites were discovered. A number of those along the eastern shore have since been reconstructed by the Welsh Water Authority and can now be viewed by following a self-guided trail about 2 miles in length. A guide-leaflet is available from the visitor centre near the western end of the dam.

The earliest site excavated was a Mesolithic campsite, the position of which is marked by a large stone, but the most impressive monuments are the Bronze Age round barrows. Four main types of barrow are represented and a ring cairn, a platform cairn, a kerb cairn and several bowl barrows have been restored for display. Seen in this condition it is easier to appreciate the original appearance of examples elsewhere. The trail also includes a number of deserted medieval settlements and enclosures.

Reconstructed ring cairn and barrow at the Brenig Bronze Age cemetery

The King's Men, Rollright Stones, Oxfordshire, was originally a ring of about 20 tall stones which formed a perfect circle

The Capel Garmon Long Barrow, Gwynedd, of middle Neolithic date, stands in a lofty position close to Snowdonia

Rituals within the Barclodiad y Gawres tomb on the Isle of Anglesey

The Penrhosfeilw standing stones are amongst the many monuments surviving on Holy Island, Anglesey, Gwynedd

The model of the Bronze Age settlement at Flag Fen, Cambridgeshire   Inset: *A preserved doorstep at Flag Fen*

BRYNCELLI DDU, *near Llanfair P G, Anglesey, Gwynedd. NGR: SH 508702*
Set among farmland in south-east Anglesey, the site is approached from the south-west along a narrow track (signposted). In its first phase, about 3000BC, Bryncelli Ddu was a henge monument. The ditch, still partly visible, enclosed an area 21m in diameter and was originally about 5.1m wide and 2m

Inside the Bryncelli Ddu tomb

deep. Within the henge was a circle of 14 free-standing stones (one survives), some with deposits of burnt human bones and quartz pebbles at their feet. In the centre was a pit in which a fire had been lit and a human ear-bone placed. A stone decorated with meandering wavy lines stood next to the pit, its position now marked by a concrete replica.

Some time later the henge was replaced by a developed passage grave, now partly restored. A grassy mound covers the interior of the former henge and part of the ditch. It was built of earth and stone, and was originally edged all around with a double kerb of upright slabs. The mound also covered the standing stone but this stone has been left visible in the reconstruction we see today.

A stone doorway in the side of the mound leads underground to a polygonal chamber. Within the chamber is a round free-standing stone pillar

whose significance is not known. One of the wall-stones in the chamber is decorated with a single spiral. Other notable features include the bench along the north side of the passage and the two upright stones set in niches on the left as you enter. Burials in the chamber included the remains of both burnt and unburnt human corpses.

About 2500BC the tomb was deliberately blocked by filling the outer passage with soil and stones. Beyond the blocking was the burial of an ox, but its date is not known.
CADW—WELSH HISTORIC MONUMENTS

CAPEL GARMON LONG BARROW, *near Betws-y-coed, Gwynedd. NGR: SH 818543*

This middle Neolithic chambered long barrow constructed in the Cotswold-Severn tradition stands at about 245m above sea level and commands spectacular views of the Snowdonia uplands. The trapezoidal cairn is 42.6m long. There is a well-defined forecourt with a false portal at the east end, and a triple chamber in the body of the mound with access from the south side.
CADW—WELSH HISTORIC MONUMENTS

Interesting constructional detail at Capel Garmon

CERRIG DUON, *near Glyntawe, Powys.*
NGR: SN 852206
This group of Bronze Age ceremonial
monuments stands on a narrow ledge or
platform overlooking the River Tawe. It
is best approached across open country
from the south-west, a walk of
approximately 2 miles.

Maen Mawr, a standing stone, is
the dominant feature of the complex and
is skilfully set to be seen along the axis
of the valley for some distance. It stands
about 1.8m high, and like the other
stones in the group is of local sandstone.

To the south of Maen Mawr is a
stone circle containing some 20 uprights,
although most are rather small. About
22m east of Maen Mawr is an avenue
comprising two slightly divergent rows
of upright stones some 4.8m apart at its
south-western end. The western side of
the avenue has 16 stones spread over a
distance of 45m; the eastern side has
only 11 stones along 24.6m. Curiously,
the avenue is not aligned on either the
stone circle or the standing stone.

Perhaps this is because they are of
different date, or perhaps the avenue
was aligned on some feature that has
now vanished.

CLEGYR BOIA, *near St David's, Dyfed.*
NGR: SM 737251
The rocky summit of this steep-sided hill
on the coastal plain of south-west Dyfed
was first occupied in early Neolithic
times, and is one of the largest
settlements of the period in Wales.

About 3800BC, at least two
rectangular houses stood on the hilltop.
Their occupants were probably cattle
farmers, and in addition to the large
quantity of pottery recovered there were
flint tools and polished stone axeheads
made from locally outcropping rocks.
Whether this settlement was defended is
not known, but in Iron Age times a
substantial rampart, which still stands
1m high, encircled most of the hilltop.
The entrance, fortified with a long
entrance tunnel, lay at the south-west
corner of the site.

Legend attributes the site to Boia,
an Irish pirate of the 6th century AD.
Boia's wife apparently sacrificed her
stepdaughter Dunawd to heathen gods
but on the same night Boia himself was
slain by a second pirate, named Lisci,
and his castle was consumed by fire
from heaven.

Plan of site at Cerrig Duon (after Grimes 1963)

DRUIDS' CIRCLE, *Cefn Coch,*
Penmaenmawr, Gwynedd.
NGR: SH 723746

This stone circle, probably the most
impressive in Wales, lies on open
moorland at a height of about 395m
above sea level. It is of the embanked
type, the upright stones being set along
the inner edge of a stone bank
approximately 0.4m high, up to 1.7m
wide and 25m in diameter.

Ten stones now remain upright and
a further 20 or so are fallen or displaced.
The entrance to the circle, marked by a
break in the bank, lies on the south-west
side. Excavations in 1958 revealed that in
the centre was a stone-lined cist in
which there was a food vessel covering
the cremated remains of a child aged
about 12. Another cist nearby also
contained the cremated remains of a
child, aged about 13, in this case
accompanied by a food vessel and a
bronze knife.

Numerous Bronze Age cairns and
small stone circles may be seen on the
moorland around the Druids' Circle. To
the north-west is the **Graig Lwyd Axe
Factory** where polished stone axes for
distribution all over Britain were made
in the centuries between approximately
4000BC and 2800BC.

DYFFRYN ARDUDWY LONG
BARROW, *near Barmouth, Gwynedd.*
NGR: SH 588228

Set on a hillside above the narrow
coastal plain, this Neolithic burial
monument, partly restored, shows two
phases of construction. Early in the
Neolithic, probably around 4200BC, a
portal dolmen comprising a stone
chamber set within a small round
mound was built. The entrance to the
chamber was completely closed, but just

*A burial at the Dyffryn Ardudwy portal dolmen as it
would have been about 3000BC*

in front of it was a small pit containing
broken pottery.

Sometime later, probably about
3700BC, the monument was enlarged. A
new rectangular cairn 30.5m long and
nearly 15m wide was built over the top
of, and partly covering, the portal
dolmen. A larger chamber, which you
can still enter, was built to the east of
the earlier one. The cremated remains of
at least one individual were found in this
later chamber.

Other Neolithic tombs in the area
include **Bron-y-foel Isaf** cairn *[NGR:
SH 608246]*, while in **Llanbedr Church**
[NGR: SH 585269] there is a stone
bearing a spiral groove like those at
Bryncelli Ddu (page 61) and Barclodiad
y Gawres (page 56).
*CADW—WELSH HISTORIC
MONUMENTS*

FFRIDD FALDWYN, *Montgomery,*
Powys. NGR: SO 217969
Situated on a prominent hill overlooking
Montgomery, this site was occupied in
Neolithic and Iron Age times. The
hillfort which now dominates the hill
began its long history in the 4th century
BC when an oval enclosure bounded by
a double palisade was constructed.
Nothing is visible of this because shortly
afterwards it was replaced by what is
now the inner circuit of defences, a
timber-laced rampart surrounded by two
outer ditches. This small fort certainly
saw action because its rampart was
burnt to a vitrified state.

During the 1st century BC a stone-
faced outer rampart was added and the
gateways at both the east and west ends

The Roman advance into Wales ended Ffridd Faldwyn's
long-standing role as a hilltop refuge

were greatly strengthened. Shortly
before the Roman Conquest the site was
hurriedly repaired, but it appears
nonetheless to have been captured and
thereafter occupation ceased.

FOEL FENLLI, *near Ruthin, Clwyd.*
NGR: SJ 163601
This site is probably the most impressive
Iron Age hillfort on the Clwydian Hills
of north Wales. Its design and
construction are more similar to the
hillforts of southern England than those
of north-west Wales, perhaps because its
builders were in close contact with
communities to the south and east.

The whole hilltop is enclosed by a
massive bank serving as an inner
rampart (which in part was made from
an inner quarry ditch), a steeply sloping
berm and an outer ditch. Around the
western half of the hill there is a small
counterscarp bank beyond the ditch of
the inner rampart, but elsewhere this
becomes a second rampart with its own
ditch and counterscarp bank beyond.
The entrance at the west end is original
and here the rampart is turned in to
provide an entrance tunnel.

Inside the fort are the remains of at
least 20 circular house platforms,
although they are often obscured by
heather. There is also a spring.

Occupation continued into the
Roman period. Legend records that the
hill takes its name from the tyrannical
King Benlli who opposed St Germanus
in the mid-5th century AD and was
consequently consumed, along with his
city, by fire from heaven.

Other Iron Age hillforts on the
Clwydian Hills include: **Moel y Gaer,**
Bodfari [NGR: SJ 095708]; **Moel Arthur**
[NGR: SJ 145661]; and **Penycloddiau**
[NGR: SJ 129677].

GWERNVALE LONG BARROW,

Crickhowell, Powys. NGR: SO 211192

This site is one of the most accessible of a small group of about a dozen long barrows constructed in the Cotswold-Severn tradition which cluster in the Black Mountains of south-eastern Wales. The site was almost completely excavated in 1977—8 when the main A40, which until that time cut through the site, was realigned. It has now been partly restored.

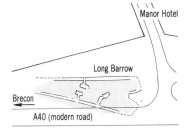

Gwernvale: plan on completion of roadbuilding (after Britnell 1984)

The earliest activity on the site was in upper Palaeolithic and Mesolithic times when a small camp was established. During the early Neolithic, about 3900BC, the site became a small farmstead, presumably occupied by a community exploiting the fertile land of the Usk Valley. These early activities probably resulted in a substantial clearing in the woodland, and this in turn may have been what attracted to the site the people who constructed the long barrow.

About 3800BC the long barrow began to be built. The trapezoidal mound was made of local sandstone rubble, carefully revetted around the edge with a fine dry-stone wall. At the south-eastern end a pair of horns flanking a small forecourt were built and a large slab of sandstone was set up to form a false entrance. The original height of the cairn is not known, but it measured 45.7m long by 17m wide.

Three chambers opened from the sides of the mound, but all had been robbed in antiquity. The tomb ceased to be used about 3100BC, and the entrances to the chambers were blocked with stones and soil to prevent the possibility of any further use.
CADW—WELSH HISTORIC MONUMENTS

HAROLD'S STONES, *Trelleck, Gwent. NGR: SO 499051*

This line of three huge blocks of local conglomerate sandstone orientated roughly north-east to south-west was probably built in Bronze Age times. Although now leaning at all angles, the stones presumably once stood upright: photographs taken early this century show them less tilted than today. The largest stone is 3.3m tall. Only the middle stone appears to have been shaped in any way, and this slab also bears two small but distinctive hollows known as cup-marks.

The tipsy Harold's Stones once presumably stood upright

HOLY ISLAND, *Anglesey, Gwynedd.*
Concentrated on and around this small
rocky island off the west coast of
Anglesey is an interesting sequence of
Neolithic, Bronze Age and Iron Age
monuments and burial chambers.

The restored Trefignath burial chamber

The earliest is the **Trefignath Long
Barrow** *[NGR: SH 258805]* south-east of
Holyhead. This tomb, fully excavated
between 1977 and 1979 and now
restored, shows three constructional
stages in its long history of use. Even
before building work on the tomb began,
the site had been occupied by an early
Neolithic community.

At first the Trefignath tomb
comprised a simple passage grave with a
small single chamber surrounded by a
round cairn. The chamber opens to the
north through a short passage formed
by two large orthostats.

In the second stage a simple
rectangular chamber was constructed
immediately east of the earlier structure.
The new chamber was surrounded by a
wedge-shaped cairn, completely
engulfing the earlier monument. A
deeply recessed forecourt providing
access to the chamber was built at the

east end. The forecourt together with the
sides of the cairn were retained by dry-
stone walling.

Finally, the third stage involved the
building of a new chamber in the
forecourt of the second-stage tomb,
together with the extension of the cairn
eastwards to surround the new chamber.
Like its predecessor, this third chamber
was rectangular in plan. Particularly
notable is the way the portal orthostats
rise above the level of the capstones to
form a monumental entrance.
Altogether, these three phases must
have spanned five or six centuries.
Inhumation was probably the main
burial rite throughout.

Other Neolithic tombs on Anglesey
include: **Barclodiad y Gawres** (page 56);
Bryncelli Ddu (page 61); **Bodowyr,**
Llanidan [NGR: SH 462681]; **Din Dryfol,**
Aberffraw [NGR: SH 395724]; **Lligwy
Burial Chamber,** *Penrhos Lligwy [NGR:
SH 501861]*; **Presaddfed Burial Chamber,**
Bodedern [NGR: SH 347809]; and **Ty
Newydd,** *Llanfaelog [NGR: SH 344738]*.

About ½ mile north-west of
Trefignath long barrow is the **Trefignath
Standing Stone** *[NGR: SH 254809]*, a fine
example of its type, 2.7m tall, probably
of Bronze Age date. At **Penrhosfeilw**
[NGR: SH 227809] are a pair of standing
stones. Both are over 3m tall and they
stand about 3.3m apart. Although they
have never been properly excavated, a
cist containing bones, arrowheads and a
spearhead was found between them
sometime last century. The purpose of
these standing stones is not known, but
they may be markers for cemeteries.

During the Iron Age, Holy Island
was densely occupied. At the **Ty Mawr
Settlement** *[NGR: SH 212820]* to the
south of Holyhead Mountain are the
remains of a small village or hamlet

The Ty Mawr Iron Age Settlement occupied a commanding viewpoint

occupied from middle Bronze Age times through into the Roman period. Some of the houses, of which only the foundations survive today, were set within individual compounds, many of them undergoing several phases of rebuilding and modification during the time of their use.

North-east of the open settlement is **Caer y Twr** *[NGR: SH 219831]*, an Iron Age hillfort of about 7ha situated on the rocky summit of Holyhead Mountain. It was probably only used as a refuge in times of trouble because few signs of occupation have been found within it. The defences are, however, most impressive.

The rampart wall has been carefully contoured to run along the top of the steepest slopes, taking in several bastion-like crags in its course. In places it still stands to a height of 3m, and it has an average thickness of 3.3m. It is constructed of dry-stone masonry with a rubble core. There is only one entrance, at the north-east corner.

Although not an archaeological monument in the strict sense,

The foundations of the Ty Mawr hut circles are still clearly visible

consideration of the Iron Age in this corner of Anglesey would not be complete without mention of **Llyn Cerrig Bach,** a small peat bog near Llanfairyneubwll *[NGR: SH 306765]* on mainland Anglesey. It was in this bog that over 100 pieces of the finest quality late Iron Age metalwork known in Wales were discovered during the construction of the Valley RAF station in 1943. The objects are now displayed in the National Museum of Wales in Cardiff. They were all probably votive offerings thrown into what was then a lake. Among the best pieces are the swords, spears, shields, horse harnesses, cart fittings, tools and ornaments.

NEVERN VALLEY AND MYNYDD PRESELI, *Dyfed*

Scattered throughout this picturesque area are a variety of prehistoric monuments ranging from the tombs of Neolithic farmers through to the hillforts and enclosures of the Iron Age.

The striking Pentre Ifan cromlech, in the Preseli foothills

Near the coast is the early Neolithic portal dolmen of **Carreg Coitan,** *Newport [NGR: SN 062393].* Recently restored, this is one of about seven similar tombs in the Nevern Valley. It has four large upright stones supporting the wedge-shaped capstone. The portal stones on the south-east side of the monument are taller than the other supports, and this, coupled with the shape of the capstone, enhances the appearance of the front of the monument. The chamber is small, about 3m square, and was originally surrounded by a roughly circular cairn.

On the high ground about 3 miles south-east of Newport is **Pentre Ifan** *[NGR: SN 099370],* also partly restored. Like many Neolithic tombs it has at least two phases of construction. First, a large

portal dolmen entirely typical of its type was erected. The portal is very splendid, with the classic H-shaped setting of stones at the front, a high closing slab across the bar of the H, and a very large wedge-shaped capstone nearly 1.5m thick at the front. Today, the capstone is supported at the back by a pointed upright, but originally there were also side stones. The chamber is large, covering some 5.5 square metres, and was built in a shallow pit. A small, low, square-shaped cairn, 15.5m long by 14.9m wide, perhaps with two projecting horns and a semicircular forecourt in the front of the portal, completed the early phase of the structure.

About 3300BC the tomb was elaborated and extended to what we see today. A façade of large stones was erected in the forecourt, and the mound was extended northwards to a total length of about 36.5m. When excavated in 1936—7 no trace of any burials was found, suggesting that the tomb had either been robbed in antiquity or that the acid soil on the site had dissolved any bones that were once present.

Late Neolithic and Bronze Age monuments are also well represented in the area. At **Cerrig y Gof** *[NGR: SN 037389]* between Newport and Dinas is an unusual type of monument which probably dates to about 2500BC. It comprises a roughly circular mound in which are set five rectangular chambers, the largest being about 2.4m by 1.8m by 1.5m. Charcoal, pottery, bones and pebbles have been found within the chambers, but the site has never been properly investigated.

The fine igneous and metamorphic rocks of Mynydd Preseli were used for making polished stone axes of various kinds throughout the later Neolithic and early Bronze Age. The famous bluestones at Stonehenge (page 41) also came from this area, and careful study of the stones themselves has pinpointed their source to the outcrops of spotted dolerite at **Carn Meini** [NGR: SN 1432]. Why such massive effort should have been dedicated to the transportation of these stones across land and sea, a distance of over 135 miles as the crow flies, is not known.

South-west of Carn Meini is the **Gors-fawr** stone circle [NGR: SN 134294]. Sixteen stones still stand in this circle which has a diameter of about 22.3m. Two large stones to the north-east of the circle may be related.

In Iron Age times south-western Wales was a largely pastoral area, and the impressive hillfort at **Foeldrygarn** on the north-eastern end of Mynydd Preseli [NGR: SN 158336] was a stronghold of the period. The centre of the hill is dominated by three large Bronze Age cairns, but around about are numerous hut platforms. The defences comprise a main inner enclosure, a second enclosure representing an extension on the north and east sides, and beyond this yet another annexe to the north-east. The second and third areas may represent no more than enlargements of the primary inner enclosure. All three areas are bounded by ramparts of dry-stone walling and rubble.

Characteristic of the non-hillfort Iron Age settlements in this part of Wales is **Castellhenllys*** near Eglwyswrw [NGR: SN 117391]. This site is a small promontory enclosure with steep precipices on three sides and a double rampart to provide defence on the fourth side. Much of the site has been excavated and restored. Two large wooden round houses have been reconstructed in their original position, and during the summer months (late May to mid-September) when the site is open to visitors (see page 116) there are all sorts of displays and experiments taking place, including traditional cooking and weaving.

Castellhenllys paints a convincing picture of life, Iron Age-style

PARC CWM LONG BARROW,

near Penmaen, West Glamorgan.
NGR: SS 537898
This partly restored middle Neolithic long barrow constructed in the Cotswold-Severn tradition stands on the floor of a narrow leafy valley well away

High on the north-east side of Parc Cwm, just beyond the long barrow, is **Cathole Cave** *[NGR: SS 538900],* which revealed evidence of occupation during upper Palaeolithic times.
CADW—WELSH HISTORIC MONUMENTS

The well-preserved Parc Cwm Long Barrow

from the busier parts of the Gower coast. The most striking feature of the site is the characteristic wedge-shaped cairn, revetted all round by a fine dry-stone wall. It is constructed of limestone rubble and today looks very much like it must have done in Neolithic times because the bare rock has not yet been colonised by grass and flowers.

At the southern end of the cairn is a bell-shaped forecourt flanked by broad horns. Part of the eastern horn was disturbed by a river flowing past the site at some time since the Neolithic period. The entrance to the burial chambers lies at the back of the forecourt; there are two pairs of side chambers leading off a central passage. Large orthostats form the walls of the passage and chamber but unfortunately the roof has been removed in antiquity and has not been restored. Excavations in 1869 recovered the remains of between 20 and 24 individuals from within the chambers.

RHOSYBEDDAU, *near Llanrhaeadr-ym-Mochnant, Powys. NGR: SJ 059303*
This Bronze Age stone circle and avenue occupies a shelf on the side of a steep valley overlooking Afon Disgynfa. The stone circle, with a diameter of about 12.8m, is accurately laid out, but only its eastern half is well preserved. Twelve stones remain standing, none more than 0.7m high.

The avenue, which lies east of the circle, is preserved for a distance of 49.3m, but how much has been lost, if any, is not known. The roughly parallel stone rows are about 3m apart. Most of the stones are fairly small, none over 0.4m tall, and they are irregular in shape. The north row is less well preserved than the south.

The avenue is orientated roughly east to west, but as at Cerrig Duon (page 62), it neither meets the circle nor does it line up with its centre. About 45m beyond the avenue to the north-east are the remains of a round cairn.

ST LYTHANS LONG BARROW, *near Barry, South Glamorgan. NGR: ST 101723*

Set on gently sloping ground amid lush pasture, this Neolithic long barrow constructed in the Cotswold-Severn tradition is dominated by its massive

St Lythans Long Barrow stands amongst green fields in the pastoral Vale of Glamorgan

stone chamber. The mound, which probably never fully covered the chamber, is aligned east to west and measures about 27m by 11m. It is rectangular in outline, and in this respect seems very similar to the Tinkinswood mound described next.

The chamber, set at the east end of the mound, is formed of three massive uprights roofed with a single capstone that is pitched upwards slightly to the east. All the stones were probably obtained locally. Although the site has never been properly excavated, human remains and coarse pottery were apparently found here in 1875.

CADW—WELSH HISTORIC MONUMENTS

TINKINSWOOD LONG BARROW, *near Barry, South Glamorgan. NGR: ST 092733*

This partly restored Neolithic long barrow lies about 1 mile north of the St Lythans barrow (see previous entry). It is approached from the east across fields by way of a footpath (signposted). The mound, roughly rectangular in plan and now a little overgrown in places, is about 40m long and 17.8m wide. It is composed of limestone rubble, and is neatly revetted on all sides by a dry-stone wall. At the eastern end is a shallow funnel-shaped forecourt flanked by two slightly flattened horns. The wall of the forecourt is rather unusual in that the stones are set at an angle in what is known as herringbone style.

The chamber, which is roomy and can still be entered, opens almost directly out of the rear of the forecourt. The walls are of large orthostats with dry-stone walling filling the gaps between the main uprights. The massive capstone measures 7.1m long, 4.5m wide, and is up to 0.9m thick. Its weight is estimated at 40 tons.

Excavations in 1914 uncovered the remains of at least 50 individuals in a jumbled state in the main chamber. Of these at least eight were children, 21 were adult females, and 16 were adult males. Some pottery was also found in the chamber.

About half-way down the mound on the north side is a polygonal cist. At the time of the excavation this was thought to be a later addition to the barrow, but an alternative theory is that it is the remains of a small early Neolithic tomb that preceded the construction of the long barrow.

CADW—WELSH HISTORIC MONUMENTS

TRE'R CEIRI, *Llanaelhaern, Gwynedd.*
NGR: SH 373446
Situated on the exposed boulder-strewn mountain peak of Yr Eifl at nearly 490m above sea level, this site, which is sometimes known as 'the town of the giants', is probably the best preserved Iron Age hillfort in Wales. It is most easily approached by footpath leading north-west from the B4417, though prospective visitors should note that reaching the site involves a steep climb.

of about 100. In the late Iron Age, or possibly later still, the number of houses increased to over 150 and the defences were reinforced by the addition of an outer wall on the north and west sides.

On fine days there are dramatic views from this site in all directions, but as the clouds gather over the mountains and the wind whistles around the exposed walls of this hilltop ghost town it is easy to imagine the inhabitants closing the doors of their houses tight and stoking up their fires.

Tre'r Ceiri, magnificently situated on rugged Yr Eifl

The earliest feature on the hill is the large cairn, probably of Bronze Age date, which stands on the summit and seems to have been respected by later occupants of the site. The first enclosure was constructed during the middle Iron Age and is now visible as the main inner wall which in places still stands to a height of 3.9m. It is constructed of dry-stone walling and traces of the original parapet and rampart walk can be seen on the north side.

There are five gateways, the two larger ones now ruinous but the three narrow ones (posterns) have straight-sided openings less than 1m wide. The north-west gate and the north postern give access to springs. Within this early enclosure there were about 20 large round houses, suggesting a population

Y GAER FAWR, *Carn Goch, near Llangadog, Dyfed. NGR: SN 691243*
This large Iron Age hillfort on the western edge of the Black Mountain has a single stone rampart and covers about 10ha. Although ruinous in parts, four postern gates and the main entrance at the north-east end can be clearly seen, all lined with upright slabs. The defences on the south-west side are particularly impressive as the rampart is nearly 19.8m thick at this point.

Inside, a single hut circle can be seen near the rampart on the south-east side. There are also later (possibly post-Roman) enclosures and a cairn of unknown date. Outside the fort to the south-east are a number of enclosures which may possibly be contemporary with the site.

CENTRAL ENGLAND AND EAST ANGLIA

Defences at Mam Tor hillfort

*T*his area contains many different types of landscape, and a variety of ancient monuments. In the west, on the uplands of the Welsh Marches, there are some of the finest hillforts, long barrows, stone circles and linear earthworks in England. Similar monuments can also be found on the southern Pennines in Derbyshire.

In the Midlands, recent agricultural activity and urban expansion mean that there is relatively little to see in the way of spectacular field monuments except for the occasional hillfort. East Anglia has been badly affected by modern agriculture, and most of the above-ground remains are in areas such as Breckland where agriculture has not been so intensive.

Recent surveys of the Fens have shown that important archaeological sites exist below the peat and alluvium which cover this area; one such site, Flag Fen in Cambridgeshire, which is open to the public, is described in this section.

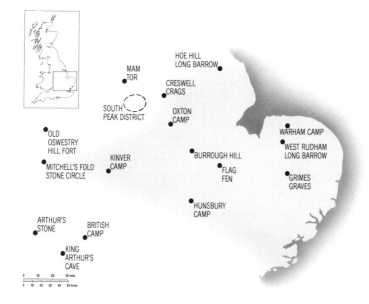

HOE HILL LONG BARROW

MAM TOR

CRESWELL CRAGS

SOUTH PEAK DISTRICT

OXTON CAMP

WARHAM CAMP

OLD OSWESTRY HILL FORT

WEST RUDHAM LONG BARROW

KINVER CAMP

BURROUGH HILL

MITCHELL'S FOLD STONE CIRCLE

FLAG FEN

GRIMES GRAVES

HUNSBURY CAMP

ARTHUR'S STONE

BRITISH CAMP

KING ARTHUR'S CAVE

0 10 20 30 mls
0 10 20 30 40 50 kms

ARTHUR'S STONE, *near Bredwardine, Hereford and Worcester. NGR: SO 318431*
This partly restored middle Neolithic long barrow, constructed in the Cotswold-Severn tradition, lies on the northern edge of a narrow upland ridge, and commands fine views over the upper Wye Valley. The mound, orientated roughly north to south, is now just a low grassy bump partly obscured by the modern road. Originally, it would have been over 26m long and up to 3m high.

The chamber, now standing naked without the mound that once covered it, has nine orthostats forming the walls and supporting the large capstone. Two stones south of the chamber may be the remains of a peristalith around the former mound. A short passage provides access to the chamber from the north-west; between the passage and chamber, and bridging the different orientations of the two parts of the structure, a small antechamber can be seen.
ENGLISH HERITAGE

BRITISH CAMP, *Little Malvern, Hereford and Worcester. NGR: SO 760399*
Occupying a prominent peak on the Malvern Hills, this massive Iron Age hillfort commands extensive views over the Severn Valley, Midland Plain and southern Welsh Marches. Constructed in several phases, the earliest earthworks are those at the centre of the site which enclose the highest part of the hill. The hillfort originally comprised a single bank and ditch with entrances to the north-east and south-west, though part of the circuit was obliterated by the 12th-century medieval castle which crowns the hill.

Above: *British Camp's defences*
Below: *Huge slabs at Arthur's Stone*

Late in the Iron Age the primary fort was expanded to enclose the whole ridge, an area of nearly 13ha. On the west side these later defences merge with the earlier ones, but elsewhere they are quite distinct and lie well outside the inner line. There are four entrances to the later Iron Age fort, on the north-east, west, east and south-east sides. Within the defences there are numerous scooped platforms, presumably the sites of houses and other buildings.

BURROUGH HILL, *near Somerby, Leicestershire. NGR: SK 761119*

This Iron Age hillfort of about 4.8ha is bounded by a single massive bank, ditch and counterscarp bank. The ramparts follow the edge of a steep-sided hilltop, and excavations have revealed that the main bank was originally faced with dry-stone walling. The entrance lies in the south-east corner where the ramparts turn sharply inwards to form a deep entrance passage nearly 46m long. At the inner end a pair of guard chambers provided extra protection for the main gates.

Excavations in the interior revealed evidence of intense occupation, large areas being given over to the storage of grain in deep rock-cut pits. Bones of pigs, sheep and cattle together with remains of querns (stone hand mills for grinding corn) suggest that the site drew on the produce of many small farmsteads in the neighbourhood.

Although established in the 2nd century BC or earlier, the site was certainly occupied in late Iron Age times and must have been one of the strongholds of the Coritani tribe — whose territory included Leicestershire and Lincolnshire — at the time of the Roman Conquest.

CRESWELL CRAGS*, *Creswell, Derbyshire. NGR: SK 535742*

Creswell Crags is a deep, narrow limestone gorge in which there are over 24 caves and rock shelters all around the base of the precipitous walls. Many of these caves were occupied for short periods at various times between the middle Palaeolithic and the present day.

Creswell Crags' long history of occupation is explained at the site's visitor centre

A visitor centre and picnic site at the north-east end of the gorge houses a display explaining the significance of the sites (see page 116), and there is a self-guided trail through the gorge starting at the visitor centre. Entry to the caves is not permitted, but grills have been fitted to the entrances so you can see in.

The main period of occupation was during upper Palaeolithic times when small groups of hunter-gatherers periodically used the gorge for seasonal camps. Among the more unusual finds are several pieces of decorated animal bone, and the remains of many now-extinct species of animals.

FLAG FEN*, *Peterborough,*
Cambridgeshire. NGR: TL 227989
The Bronze Age settlement in Flag Fen
was a huge artificial island covering over
0.8ha. It was set within what was then a
lagoon, and linked to dry land by a
timber walkway. Since its discovery in
1982, about 2 per cent of the island has
been excavated to reveal the roof
supports and timber walls of a large
rectangular building over 18m long. The
floors contained broken pottery
fragments, animal bones and cereal
grains. Sand had been spread on the
floor in Bronze Age times to counteract
the damp.

A visitor centre at the site, usually
open daily from Easter through to
October (see page 116), contains a
permanent exhibition which includes the
wooden remains of the large Bronze Age
house and a large-scale model of the
site itself.

GRIMES GRAVES*, *near Thetford,*
Norfolk. NGR: TL 817898
Set deep among the conifer plantations
of the Breckland, this is the largest and
best-known group of Neolithic flint
mines in Britain, and the only site at
which you can actually go down into
one of the old mines. Grimes Graves
was worked for flint between about
3000BC and 1900BC, and traces of over
600 shafts are known. Several shafts
have been excavated, and found to be up
to 14m deep.

One of the shafts, about 9m deep,
has been made safe for public access.
Today you climb down into the mine by
way of a vertical metal ladder, but the
original miners had only ropes and tree
trunks with steps cut into one side.
Once at the bottom you can see galleries
radiating out from the main shaft. You
cannot go into these galleries, but by
crouching down and looking into the
gloom beyond the modern grills it is
easy to visualise Neolithic miners
crouching in the narrow tunnels prising
out flint nodules with antler picks and
wooden levers.

*Section through a mineshaft at Grimes Graves. Miners
are digging galleries and carrying flints and waste chalk
to the surface*

Then look at the shaft itself. It has
been estimated that six or seven people
would have to work for 32 consecutive
days to dig out the solid chalk, and then
work a further 13 days to extract the flint
from the base of the shaft and the
galleries. Each shaft would have yielded
about 8 tons of flint, and after being
quarried it would have been taken up to
the surface and made into a variety of
tools including axes and knives.
ENGLISH HERITAGE (see page 116)

One of the Devil's Arrows, North Yorkshire, standing stones that may have been linked with fertility rituals

Bones of prehistoric animals were discovered in the Victoria Cave, North Yorkshire. As the reconstruction depicts, these caves would once have provided shelter for groups of hunters

The eight upright stones at Cairnholy, Dumfries and Galloway.
Inset: *The fascinating Jarlshof site, Shetland, was discovered thanks to a savage storm in 1897*

Midsummer sunrise at the Callanish standing stones, Western Isles

Orkney's Skara Brae site tells us a great deal about late Neolithic domestic life

HOE HILL LONG BARROW, *near Binbrook, Lincolnshire. NGR: TF 215953*
This fine middle Neolithic long barrow was constructed in the earthen long barrow tradition. The mound measures 54.8m long by 18.2m wide, and is orientated approximately east to west. The material used to construct it was derived from flanking quarry ditches, not now visible. A dip near the centre of the mound may have resulted from the collapse of an internal structure, or, more likely, the robbing of the mound.

Earthen long barrows differ from those of the Cotswold-Severn tradition in having a wooden mortuary structure rather than stone chambers. The burial rites are, however, broadly the same: complete bodies were first placed in the chamber entrance, and then, as the flesh decomposed, parts of the body would be moved further into the chamber until eventually the whole skeleton lay deep inside the tomb within a heap of disarticulated human remains.

Until recently there was a second long barrow at Hoe Hill only 65m to the north-west. This has now disappeared. About 1½ miles north of Hoe Hill on the opposite side of the valley of the Waithe Beck is the **Ash Hill Long Barrow** *[NGR: TF 209961]*. This mound is wedge-shaped in plan, about 39m long and 16.1m wide. Like Hoe Hill it has never been excavated.

HUNSBURY CAMP, *Northampton, Northamptonshire. NGR: SP 737584*
This Iron Age hillfort now appears as a round enclosure defended by a single bank and ditch. The ditch was originally 6.7m deep, but is now largely silted up. When first constructed the bank was revetted by vertical timbers but later, during a remodelling of the defences, a

clay covering was added to make the front of the rampart slope at the same angle as the inner face of the ditch. Traces of an outer ditch were discovered in 1903, but nothing of this structure is now visible.

The interior was heavily disturbed by iron mining last century and the ground surface inside the fort has been lowered by about 2.4m. During this work, many storage pits were discovered. A large collection of Iron Age pottery, metalwork and other objects was amassed, much of it now in Northampton Museum. The site was most intensively occupied during the 1st century BC, but the hillfort was probably first established in the 4th century BC.

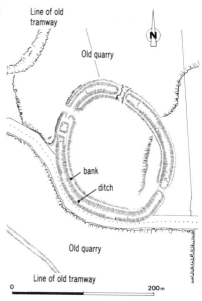

Plan of Hunsbury Camp (after Royal Commission on the Historic Monuments of England)

KING ARTHUR'S CAVE, *Whitchurch, Hereford and Worcester. NGR: SO 545155*
Situated some 90m above the present River Wye, this cave was intermittently occupied from upper Palaeolithic times until the Roman period. The cave, which can still be entered, comprises two chambers, the largest one over 16.7m

times, but claims in the national press (1981) that cave art had been discovered in the area have since proved bogus. Cave art as such is unlikely to survive in Britain because of the inclement climate, but drawings showing animals of various sorts have been found scratched on to pieces of bone.

Ashes from the fires of Stone Age hunters have been discovered outside King Arthur's Cave

deep. Both are approached by a short passage leading into the hill from a broad entrance area containing a natural pillar of rock. In front of the entrance is a broad platform which is now rather shaded by trees.

Excavations in 1870—1 revealed that the earliest occupation was deep inside the cave. The bones of mammoth, woolly rhinoceros, lion, bison and great Irish elk were found. These suggest that the cave was in use during a cold period, perhaps during the onset of the Devensian glaciation.

During the later part of the upper Palaeolithic, occupation seems to have been mostly confined to the entrance area and the platform immediately outside the cave proper. Tools and weapons of Creswellian tradition were found scattered around remains of hearths. Traces of Mesolithic, Neolithic, Bronze Age and Iron Age activity in the cave have also been recorded.

Other caves in the Wye Valley were variously occupied during Palaeolithic

KINVER CAMP, *Kinver, Staffordshire. NGR: SO 835832*
This Iron Age promontory fort lies in light woodland at the north end of a narrow sandstone ridge with wonderful views of the Clent Hills to the east and Wenlock Edge to the west. Steep slopes provide natural defence on the northwest and south-east sides, and a single massive rampart crosses the ridge to form the south side of the enclosure which in total covers about 3ha. No trace of an entrance remains.

Below the hillfort on the north side, at **Holy Austin Rock,** are a series of houses burrowed out of the soft sandstone. Some may be prehistoric in origin, but most are wholly or substantially of more recent date. Holy Austin Rock itself was a hermitage until the Reformation, and some of the others were occupied as houses until the 1950s — apparently the last troglodyte dwellings known in this country.
NATIONAL TRUST

MAM TOR, *near Castleton, Derbyshire.*
NGR: SK 128837
Overlooking the Vale of Edale, the Iron
Age hillfort of Mam Tor is situated on an
exposed hilltop at nearly 520m above sea
level. The defences, with a circumference
of nearly 1100m, consist of a single bank
constructed out of dumped rubble in
places revetted front and back with a
dry-stone wall, flanked on the outside
by a ditch. The rampart roughly follows
the form of the hill, enclosing an area of
6.4ha. Excavations in 1965—7 revealed
that on the eastern side the bank was
5.4m wide and 3m high.

Two entrances have been
identified. At the south entrance the
rampart is turned in to form a narrow
approach passage nearly 30m long; on
the north side a similar arrangement
may be noted but the passage here is
only 15m long.

Excavations in the interior revealed
a number of circular houses constructed
on levelled platforms terraced into the
hillside. Radiocarbon dates on material
from these houses put them firmly in
the late Bronze Age, but whether the
defences are equally early is not known.
NATIONAL TRUST

The lofty defences at Mam Tor in the Peak District

MITCHELL'S FOLD STONE CIRCLE, *near Chirbury, Shropshire. NGR: SO 305984*

This Bronze Age stone circle lies on open moorland towards the south-western end of Stapeley Hill with extensive views to both east and west over the Severn Valley and Welsh hills.

Fourteen stones remain standing, all less than 2m tall and the majority less than 1m tall. The circle has a diameter of about 25m but the remaining stones are irregularly spaced. About 75m to the south-east is a very weathered stone set on a small cairn. Legend records that a tenant of the land on which the circle stands once removed one of the stones to use in his cowshed, but later that night he became so alarmed by a thunderstorm that next day he replaced the stone.

About 2 miles south of Mitchell's Fold, but clearly visible from the site, is **Corndon Hill** *[NGR: SO 3096]*. Fine volcanic rock known as Hyssington picrite was quarried from the south end of this hill in late Neolithic and early Bronze Age times to make polished tools and weapons.
ENGLISH HERITAGE

OLD OSWESTRY HILLFORT, *Oswestry, Shropshire. NGR: SJ 296310*

This impressive Iron Age hillfort is one of the most outstanding monuments in the Welsh Marches and commands very fine views over the valley of the River Dee. The defences are preserved as a series of grass-covered banks and silted-up ditches but, coupled with what is known from excavations, they tell the story of the monument very clearly.

Plan of Mitchell's Fold Stone Circle

0   10   20   30 m

Wave upon wave of undulations at Old Oswestry Hillfort, the grassy imprint of Iron Age defences. In common with many other hillforts, Old Oswestry was improved, strengthened and enlarged over the centuries

The earliest settlement on the hill comprised a group of undefended round houses. Construction of the hillfort probably began in the 5th century BC with the building of the two innermost ramparts: an inner bank revetted front and back with a stone wall, a ditch, a second rampart of dumped soil and rubble, and another ditch beyond. The area enclosed was rectangular, and there were entrances to the east and west.

In the second phase the inner bank was enlarged and a third bank and ditch were added all around except on the south-east side where the steep natural slope made additional defences unnecessary. Finally, two further ramparts were constructed around the hill (the outermost pair) except on the south-east side where just one line was added. The eastern entrance was also strengthened at this time.

Occupation was intense during Iron Age times, but the site was seemingly abandoned after the Roman Conquest. Several centuries later the earthwork boundary between Mercia and Wales known as Wat's Dyke was carried right up to the Iron Age ramparts on both the north and south sides. *ENGLISH HERITAGE*

OXTON CAMP, *Oxton, Nottinghamshire. NGR: SK 635532*

This small Iron Age hillfort covering less than 0.4ha was defended by three lines of banks and ditches on the east side and by a single rampart comprising a bank, ditch and counterscarp bank around the remainder of the circuit. An original entrance can be seen on the north-west side but less certainly ancient is the gap in the south-east side.

Outside the north-west entrance is a large round barrow, probably of Bronze Age date, known rather inexplicably as **Robin Hood's Pot.** It is over 27.5m in diameter and some 6m high. Roman coins and evidence of an early medieval burial have been discovered at this site.

SOUTH PEAK DISTRICT, *Derbyshire*
Middle and late Neolithic tombs are
scattered throughout the southern Peak
District. At **Green Low,** *near Grangemill
[NGR: SK 232580]*, the remains of a
robbed oval cairn, 18.8m by 15.8m, can
be seen. At the south-eastern end of the
cairn is a straight façade, opening from
its centre into a rectangular chamber
subdivided into two cells. The walls of
the chamber are made of large slabs of
local limestone. Burials in this tomb
were probably by inhumation, but the
site was robbed in Roman times.

To the north-west is **Bee Low,** *near
Youlgreave [NGR: SK 192647]*, a round
cairn about 12.1m across and 1.5m high.
Excavations between 1966 and 1968
revealed that it was constructed during
the early Bronze Age, about 2500BC,
and used over a period of perhaps three
centuries. The earliest burials were a
group of six skeletons placed together in
a central cist along with a very fine
beaker pot. Other cists were found
elsewhere in the mound, along with the
remains of three cremations.

Another early Bronze Age barrow
can be seen at **Hob Hurst's House,** *near
Baslow [NGR: SK 287692]*. This mound,
10m in diameter and 1.2m high, has a
ditch around it. A stone cist containing
cremated human remains was found at
the centre.

At **Gib Hill,** *Middleton [NGR: SK
158633]*, is another large round barrow,
but in this case it is possible to
distinguish two main periods in its
construction. When first built the tomb
was an oval monument 40.2m by 22.8m.
No burials are known from this period.
Later, during the early Bronze Age, a
large round mound was added to the
eastern end of the oval mound. A stone
cist some 0.7m by 0.6m was found in

this part of the monument. It contained
the cremated remains of one individual
together with a small pottery urn. The
name Gib Hill is thought to derive
from the fact that a man was hanged
on a gibbet there for a murder
committed nearby.

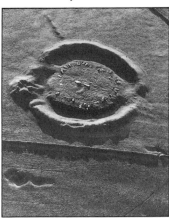

Top: *Arbor Low shares similarities with the monuments
at Stonehenge and Avebury*
Above: *Arbor Low's ceremonial stones may once have
stood upright*

North-east of Gib Hill is the great
henge of **Arbor Low** *[NGR: SK 160636]*,
one of the best-preserved henge
monuments in England. Now under
pasture, the rounded remains of the
outer bank dominate the skyline as you

approach the site. Standing on the bank gives wonderful views out over the Peak District National Park, and in some ways is reminiscent of standing on the great bank at Avebury (pages 22—3). In front of you is the partly silted-up ditch, and beyond lies the flat interior of the henge with its circle of limestone slabs around a possible 'cove'. All the stones are today flat on the ground, but they may originally have been upright as at Avebury or Stonehenge. Excavations at Arbor Low in 1901—2 revealed a human burial immediately beside the site of the possible cove.

The henge is served by two opposing entrances to the north-west and south-east, marked today by gaps in the bank and causeways across the ditch. Just outside the south-eastern entrance is a large round cairn of Bronze Age date. When excavated in 1845 it was found to contain cremations, a bone pin and two pottery food vessels, all within a stone cist. On the southern approach to the henge a low bank and ditch of uncertain age can be seen.

The henge known as **The Bull Ring,** *near Dove Holes [NGR: SK 078782]*, is similar to Arbor Low, but with no central stones remaining.

Probably the most impressive group of Bronze Age monuments in Derbyshire is on **Stanton Moor** *[centred on NGR: SK 2463]*. At the northern end is the **Nine Ladies Stone Circle** *[NGR: SK 253635]*, 10m in diameter and with nine remaining stones set on a low bank. In the centre are the remains of a small cairn, and to the south-west is a single upright stone known as the King Stone. Other remains on this history-laden moor include over 70 round barrows, at least three ring-cairns and a number of small enclosures.

The King Stone and Nine Ladies Stone Circle

About 5 miles south-west of Stanton Moor is the **Roystone Grange Trail** which begins in the *Minninglow car park [NGR: SK 195582]*. This self-guided trail, which follows fairly well-made paths, was established by the University of Sheffield and the Peak District National Park and covers a distance of about 4 miles. It takes at least 2 hours to complete the walk.

The whole area traversed by the trail was heavily settled in prehistoric times. The Neolithic barrow of **Minninglow** can be seen from the trail, and near Roystone Grange is a Bronze Age round barrow, whilst prehistoric fields have been recorded around and about. Also on the trail are the remains of a Roman farm and fieldsystem, a medieval grange and a post-medieval brick works.

WARHAM CAMP, *Warham, Norfolk.*
NGR: TF 945409
This is the best-preserved Iron Age
hillfort in Norfolk. Almost exactly
circular in plan, an area of 1.4ha is
enclosed by two massive ramparts which
are continuous except where cut by the
River Stiffkey which was diverted to its
present course in the 18th century AD.
No certain entrance has been found,
although the gap in the north-north-
west may be original.

Excavations have revealed that the
inner ditch is flat bottomed and about

The inner and outer ramparts at Warham Camp

3.3m deep. Both banks now rise 3m
above the level of the interior.
Originally, the banks were faced with
wooden revetments. Few finds were
made during the excavations, but the
site may be tentatively dated to the later
part of the Iron Age, perhaps with some
occupation continuing through into the
Roman period.

WEST RUDHAM LONG BARROW,
near Harpley, Norfolk. NGR: TF 810254
This Neolithic long barrow, constructed
in the earthen long barrow tradition, is
one of the very few examples which
survive in East Anglia. The mound, now
partly under woodland, is almost oval in
plan, 64m long by 21m wide. It is
orientated roughly north to south.

Nothing of the interior of the
monument is visible today, but
excavations in 1937—8 revealed that the
core of the mound was of turf, and that
this was covered with gravel quarried
from the ditch. The ditch, which was
generally 3.6m wide, 1.2m deep and V-
shaped in cross section, ran all the way
around the mound, close up against it
with no berm.

A small elliptical area at the south
end of the main mound was surrounded
on three sides by a fairly insubstantial
ditch. This may be the remains of an
original monument later incorporated
into the long barrow, or, alternatively, an
extension of the long barrow.

Under the south end of the main
mound was some sort of platform on
which human bodies were cremated. No
human bone was, however, discovered
because of the acidic nature of the soil.
Finds were generally poor, but did
include a leaf-shaped flint arrowhead
and a crude flint scraper from the ditch.

THE NORTH COUNTRY

The magnificent Castle Rigg Stone Circle

*D*ominated by upland areas such as the Lake District, Pennines, North York Moors and the Cheviots, the north of England contains many spectacular groups of prehistoric monuments set amid imposing landscapes. Later prehistoric monuments are particularly numerous on the uplands; Cumbria is well known for its stone circles, the Cheviots for their hillforts and enclosures dating to the Iron Age.

The lower ground was also extensively settled in prehistoric times. The Yorkshire Wolds are rich in Neolithic burial monuments, while some very fine henges cluster in the valleys of the main rivers flowing eastwards off the Pennines.

Northern England was not conquered by the Romans until the 70s AD, and even then, with the boundary of the province set along a line roughly between Newcastle upon Tyne and Carlisle, parts of northern England remained outside the Roman world.

BIRKRIGG COMMON,

near Ulverston, Cumbria.
Centred on NGR: SD 2974

Within this area of wild moorland overlooking Morecambe Bay there are at least nine Bronze Age round barrows, a stone circle and two enclosures.

Four barrows in a group [NGR: SD 286742] are typical of many in the area in being between 3.6m and 6.4m in diameter but only 0.3m high. Of the larger barrows on the common, one [NGR: SD 289743] contained three inhumations together with a small bronze awl. A rectangular barrow [NGR: SD 288746] contained seven cremations, three in urns dating to the middle Bronze Age.

The stone circle [NGR: SD 292739] is rather unusual in having two concentric rings of stones. The inner ring has 10 uprights and a diameter of 9.1m, the outer ring has 15 stones and a diameter of about 25.9m. Five human cremations have been found within the inner circle, one contained inside an inverted collared urn.

Two enclosures lie north-east and south-west of the rectangular barrow described earlier. Both are probably of Iron Age date.

THE BRIDESTONES, *near Congleton, Cheshire/Staffordshire border. NGR: SJ 906622*

Although only the chamber of this middle Neolithic long barrow now survives, records suggest that originally there was a mound over 90m long and 12m wide. Orientated east to west, the visible chamber apparently lay at the eastern end of the barrow. The chamber is rectangular in plan, 5.6m long, and divided into two parts by a slab (now

Only the bare bones now survive of the Bridestones burial chamber

broken) that is pierced by a circular hole known as a 'porthole'.

To the east of the chamber is a semicircular forecourt, the edges of which can just be traced by the line of large stones. Two further chambers are said to have been destroyed when the mound was removed in the 18th century AD.

CASTLE RIGG STONE CIRCLE,

near Keswick, Cumbria. NGR: NY 292236

Perched on its own hilltop in the heart of the Lake District above Keswick, this late Neolithic or early Bronze Age stone circle is probably one of the most magnificent examples of its type in England. In fine weather the mountains of the Lake District provide a back-drop second to none, and even when the sun is not shining the clouds seem to assemble in dramatic patterns.

The circle, which because of its one slightly flattened side is not

Mysterious and majestic: the beautifully located Castle Rigg Stone Circle

geometrically perfect, has 38 surviving stones on the outer circumference. Eight of them exceed 1.5m in height, and many seem to have a character of their own for they all consist of natural unhewn boulders.

Inside the circle on the east side is an unusual rectangular arrangement comprising 10 stones, the easternmost narrow end of the rectangle connecting with the circle. Its purpose is not known. A possible entrance gap can be seen on the northern side of the main circle, and there is an outlying stone some 90.2m away to the south-west.

The relatively close spacing of the stones at Castle Rigg, the marked entrance, and the presence of an outlier suggest that this site is early in the tradition of stone circle building and can probably be dated to between 3370BC and 2670BC.

ENGLISH HERITAGE and NATIONAL TRUST

COPT HILL ROUND BARROW,
Houghton le Spring, Tyne and Wear.
NGR: NZ 353492

This is an early or middle Neolithic round barrow over 18.2m in diameter and 2.4m high. Excavated in 1877, the mound was found to cover a rectangular structure, 10.3m by 1.8m, orientated east to west. The structure was defined on all sides by boulder walls and a large post stood at either end.

Human bodies were placed within the rectangular area. Later, when sufficient time had elapsed for the flesh to have completely decomposed, the whole deposit was cremated. The mound was constructed soon after the cremation rites were complete. During the early Bronze Age eight burials were added to the mound — one cremation contained within a collared urn and seven inhumations (including a child) accompanied by a food vessel.

THE DEVIL'S ARROWS,

Boroughbridge, North Yorkshire.
NGR: SE 391666

These are three large upright stones in a line orientated roughly north to south. The northernmost is 5.4m high and 6.7m round; the central stone, 6.8m high and 5.4m in perimeter, stands 61m to the south; the southern stone, of similar size, is a further 113m away. Originally there may have been two additional, smaller, stones but all trace of these has long since vanished.

The stones are of millstone grit which must have been brought to the site from near Knaresborough, 7 miles away. They are all natural blocks; the grooves that can now be seen result from weathering.

About 4 miles north-west of The Devil's Arrows are the henge

The Devil's Arrows: each weighs more than 20 tons

monuments at **Hutton Moor** *[NGR: SE 353736]* and **Cana** *[NGR: SE 361718]*, both surrounded by numerous round barrows. Further north-west still are the Thornborough Henges (page 99).

DODDINGTON MOOR, *near Wooler, Northumberland. Centred on NGR: NU 0031*

Overlooking the River Till, this area of moor was heavily occupied in later prehistoric times.

On the west side is **Dod Law Fort** *[NGR: NU 004317]*, a D-shaped enclosure of about 0.2ha with a small annexe to the north-west. The main enclosure has two banks of earth and stone which survive in places to a height of 2.7m. There are entrances on the north-west and south-east. The remains of several huts can be seen within the main enclosure, but there are none in the annexe, suggesting that the fort was a farmstead and animal pound built as one unit. It is probably late Bronze Age or Iron Age in date.

On the east side is **Dod Law Enclosure** *[NGR: NU 006317]*, a roughly rectangular area of about 0.6ha defined by a single bank and ditch, and possibly contemporary with the fort. Entrances lie on the north-east and south-west sides. The latter has out-turned banks forming a funnel-shaped approach such as might be found on a stock enclosure.

All over the moor are numerous boulders which bear cup-and-ring designs — small cup-like hollows connected together and/or surrounded by circular grooves. These are generally thought to be of Bronze Age date, but few have been securely dated and their purpose is not known. Another enclosure and a stone circle are located further to the east.

ESKDALE MOOR, *near Boot, Cumbria.*
Centred on NGR: NY 1702
Scattered across this area of high
moorland are five stone circles. The
largest, **Brats Hill** *[NGR: NY 173023]*, is
nearly circular and about 30m in
diameter. Most of its 42 stones are now
fallen. About 10.6m to the north-west is
a small outlier.

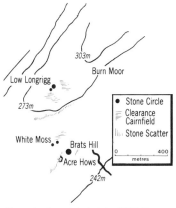

The complex of stone circles located on Eskdale Moor
(after Burl 1976)

Inside the circle there are five small
round cairns which all stand less than
0.5m high and range from about 6m to
7.5m in diameter. Originally all the
cairns were edged with a kerb of
boulders. Excavations in the early 19th
century AD revealed human cremations,
animal bones and antlers underneath the
cairns, but whether the cairns were built
before or after the construction of the
stone circle is not known. It is, however,
notable that they all lie in the southern
part of the enclosed area, four of them in
the south-west quadrant.

About 150m to the north-west of
Brats Hill are the two **White Moss Stone
Circles** *[NGR: NY 172024]*, both about
16m in diameter and both containing a

single cairn. Four hundred metres
further north are another pair of circles,
the **Low Longrigg Stone Circles** *[NGR:
NY 172028]*. One of these contains a
single cairn; the other, which is more
oval than circular in its plan, encloses
two cairns.

Just over 6 miles to the north-east,
around **Langdale Pikes** *[NGR: NY 2707]*,
are the quarries and rock faces exploited
in middle Neolithic times to obtain fine
rock for the manufacture of axes and
other edged tools which were distributed
to all parts of Britain.

Stone axe 'factories' are reputedly located in various
places on Pike of Stickle (the prominent peak on the right
of the photograph), one of the two Langdale Pikes

FIVE BARROWS, *Holystone,*
Northumberland. NGR: NT 953020
This Bronze Age cemetery of at least
nine barrows is located on sloping
ground overlooking the River Coquet.
The barrows range in size from 3.6m to
over 18.2m in diameter, and from about
0.3m to over 1.2m high. Most were
excavated during the 19th century AD
and variously found to contain either
complete human skeletons or
cremations, some accompanied by urns
or food vessels, others by bone pins or
flint tools.

South of the barrow cemetery is a
stone row known as the **Five Kings**
[NGR: NT 955015]. About 14m long, its
stones are 1.5m to 2.4m high.

GRASSINGTON, *Grassington, North Yorkshire. Centred on NGR: SD 9965*
Here we have probably the best-preserved Iron Age and Romano-British fields in northern England. Low banks and walls, in places surviving to a height of 0.9m, form the field boundaries. Around **High Close** and **Sweetside** *[NGR: SE 0065]* the ancient fields are rectangular in outline and regular in their arrangement. Most are between 106m and 121m long by about 21m wide. Hut circles can be seen within some. Further south the fields are smaller and less regular.

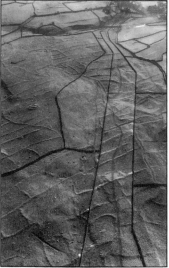

Grassington's chequer-board of fieldsystems

The largest fields are on **Lea Green** *[NGR: SD 9966]*. Most are again rectangular but here they commonly measure 150m long by 60m to 90m wide. Circular and oval enclosures up to 30m across lie within and between the fields. At the northern end of Lea Green is a well-defined village of hut-circles.

ILKLEY MOOR, *Ilkley, West Yorkshire. Centred on NGR: SE 1045*
Over 30 natural boulders decorated with carvings and cup-and-ring marks lie around the edge of Ilkley Moor. They are probably of Bronze Age date, and the carvings include concentric rings, ladder-pattern designs, wavy lines and swastikas. Some are difficult to find when the vegetation is high, but the three main concentrations are: **Rivock Group** *[NGR: SE 074447]*; **Addington Moor Group** *[NGR: SE 072465]*; and **Green Slack Group** *[NGR: SE 104470]*. How cup-and-ring marked stones were used is not clear, but in this case their location all around the edge of the moor may suggest that perhaps they somehow guard the sites which lie in the heart of the moor like symbolic magic-eyes watching out for intruders.

Hut circles, enclosures and field boundaries, all probably of Bronze Age date, can also be seen on the moor, together with cairns and ceremonial monuments of similar date.

The **Twelve Apostles** *[NGR: SE 125451]* is an embanked stone circle with 12 stones set in an earth bank approximately 15.9m in diameter. The **Grubstones Stone Circle** *[NGR: SE 136447]* is almost perfectly circular in diameter, with 20 stones still standing on a slight bank. **Horncliffe Stone Circle** *[NGR: SE 134435]* is oval in plan. Some 46 closely set stones survive around the outside, and there are also traces of an inner ring.

The largest of the many round barrows on the moor is **The Skirtful of Stones** *[NGR: SE 140445]* which measures 25.9m in diameter and still stands 1.5m high (see Barclodiad y Gawres, page 56, for possible derivation of the name).

PENRITH AREA, *Cumbria*

Long Meg casts a watchful eye over Her Daughters

The higher ground of the Lake District is dominated by monuments of Bronze Age date, but around the edge of the uplands such as in the Penrith area, there are sites which can be dated to both earlier and later periods.

Long Meg and Her Daughters [NGR: NY 571373] is a splendid Neolithic or early Bronze Age standing stone and associated stone circle lying in lush pasture not far from the River Eden. Many legends surround the origin of this site. One tells of an indignant saint who turned a local coven of witches into stones; another claims that the stones which make up the circle were Long Meg's lovers.

The circle is actually an oval setting with about 50 stones on its circumference, 27 of them still standing, although originally there may have been as many as 70. Most are large, up to 3m tall, the heaviest being a huge block at the south-south-west which is estimated to weigh some 28 tons.

Long Meg, a tall, lean standing stone with a pointed top, lies about 18m outside the circle to the south-west. It is 3.6m high, and on the north-western face are traces of three designs: a cup-and-ring mark, a spiral and some incomplete concentric circles. Unlike the outliers found at the majority of stone circles, Long Meg seems to be significantly placed in relation to the centre of the circle because its alignment is almost exactly that over which the midwinter sun would have set in late Neolithic times. What connection this event may have had with the rituals performed at the site is not known. There are two other outliers, about 8.5m apart, between Long Meg and the circle.

About ½ mile to the north-east is **Little Meg** [NGR: NY 577375], a circle of 11 stones which, when originally constructed, surrounded a barrow.

King Arthur's Round Table, *Penrith* [NGR: NY 523284], is a late Neolithic henge monument about 7 miles south-west of Long Meg and Her Daughters. Its present appearance is slightly deceptive because the site was heavily disturbed in the 19th century AD, but it is possible to see the ditch, with a diameter of about 91.4m, and the remains of the bank outside it. The berm separating the bank from ditch is a recent feature; so too is the low mound on the central plateau.

Despite 19th-century disturbance, King Arthur's Round Table still reveals its ancestry

Originally there were two opposing entrances, but only the one on the south-east side remains. Records suggest that two stones once stood outside the northernmost entrance. Excavations during the 1930s showed that the ditch was flat bottomed, 1.1m to 1.5m deep, and 9.1m wide. Within the henge a trench containing cremated human bone was discovered. It had been covered by a stone structure of some kind.

Nearby is **Mayborough Henge** [NGR: NY 519285]. This site, probably also of late Neolithic date, is unusual because it does not have a ditch inside the bank and may not therefore belong to the mainstream of henge-building in the British Isles.

The bank, constructed of stones gathered up from around about, still stands to a height of 4.5m in places and encloses an area 110m in diameter. The entrance is to the east. Near the centre is a single standing stone about 2.7m tall, the lone survivor of a group of four known to have stood within the henge in the 19th century AD. Four more stones once flanked the entrance.

Of later date is the Iron Age enclosure at **Castlesteads** [NGR: NY 518252]. An area of about 0.1ha is enclosed by three concentric banks with two ditches between them. No original entrance is visible, although one may have existed on the east side where the defences have been heavily damaged. The interior is divided into a series of small enclosures.

Rather similar is the slightly larger D-shaped enclosure in **Yanwath Wood** [NGR: NY 519260]. The defences at this site comprise two banks, possibly the remains of walls, with a ditch between them. The main entrance is to the north-west, although the gap on the south-east side might also be original. Again there are several small enclosures within the defended area.

More typical of the Iron Age hillforts in north-east England is **Dunmallet,** *near Dacre* [NGR: NY 468246] at the north end of Ullswater. Set on a conical hill with unusually steep sides, the enclosed area totals about 0.4ha. The defences comprise a single bank and ditch with traces of a counterscarp bank in places. The entrance lies to the south-west of the site.

RUDSTON AREA,

Humberside/North Yorkshire

Until relatively recently, the Yorkshire Wolds were exceptionally rich in upstanding prehistoric monuments. Intensive agriculture and quarrying have changed this, and while much is still visible the sites now survive mostly as islands in a sea of arable farmland.

Duggleby Howe *[NGR: SE 881669]* is probably the finest middle Neolithic round barrow in Britain. It is now a grass-covered tump standing near the source of the Gypsey Race, 36m in diameter and 6m high.

Man-made Duggleby Howe, unmistakable in its flat farmland setting

You cannot enter the mound, but excavations in 1890 revealed that in the centre was a rectangular shaft cut into the bedrock to a depth of nearly 3m. At the bottom was the burial of an adult male accompanied by a pot and some pieces of flint. Two other burials and a separate human skull were added as the shaft was back-filled, and two further burials were inserted into the top of the shaft, one accompanied by a flint axe, arrowhead and antler macehead, the other by a fine polished flint knife. Subsequently, a hollow was dug next to

the shaft and six bodies buried in it. A small round barrow was then erected, six infants, one adolescent and an adult being buried within the mound as it was piled up. In late Neolithic times 53 cremations were inserted into the top of this, the earliest mound.

The massive chalk rubble mound visible today was added to the initial construction later still, although exactly when is not certain. The barrow was the site of a windmill in medieval times. Aerial photography has established that Duggleby Howe lies within an incomplete enclosure bounded by a causeway ditch. Nothing of this is now visible at ground level.

The complexity of the burials at Duggleby Howe, and the fact that they accumulated over several centuries, is a feature of some, but not all, Neolithic burial monuments on the Yorkshire Wolds. At the **Wold Newton Barrow** *[NGR: TA 048726]* excavations in 1894 established that here the mound covered a wooden structure of some sort within which several human bodies had been placed. The barrow, still visible, was mostly of turf and measures 26m in diameter and 3.3m high.

Further east along the Great Wold Valley is **Willy Howe** *[NGR: TA 063724]*, another fine middle Neolithic round barrow surviving as a mound nearly 40m in diameter and 7m high. Excavations produced no certain evidence of burials, but a rock-cut shaft rather similar to the one at Duggleby Howe was located under the centre of the mound.

Middle Neolithic long barrows also occur in this part of England. The **Willerby Wold Long Barrow** *[NGR: TA 029761]* on the Humberside/North Yorkshire border has a rectangular mound 37m long by 10m wide. Constructed in the earthen long barrow tradition, excavations have revealed that this barrow covered a wedge-shaped enclosure bounded by a wooden fence. At the east end was a concave forecourt. Within the enclosure was a trench covered by a simple timber chamber of some sort. The barrow had been constructed over the top of both the enclosure and the chamber.

After several bodies had accumulated in the chamber it was set on fire. This practice is peculiar to monuments in Yorkshire and Humberside. The effect was to cremate the bodies and/or skeletons in the chamber and at the same time to prevent any further use of the tomb because, once the timber walls of the chamber had burnt through, the weight of the mound above brought the whole structure crashing down on top of the burial deposits.

A similar pattern of events was recorded during the excavation of the **Kilham Long Barrow** [NGR: TA 056673]. This mound, 52m long and 18m wide, was later reused as the setting for a Bronze Age round barrow which was added to the south-western end in approximately 2300BC.

Around the village of Rudston, aerial photography has revealed no less than four cursus monuments. Little can be seen on the ground except near **The Woldgate** [NGR: TA 099658] where the southern terminal of the easternmost cursus survives as a slight mound next to the road. Traces of the parallel ditches forming the long sides of the cursus can be seen heading northwards towards Rudston village.

The meeting of the four cursus monuments boxes in the high ground now occupied by Rudston parish church. In prehistoric times, however, this focus was marked by the massive needle-like

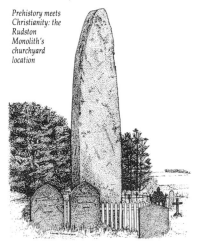

Prehistory meets Christianity: the Rudston Monolith's churchyard location

Rudston Monolith [NGR: TA 097677] which still stands beside the church. This is the tallest standing stone in Britain at 7.7m high. It is made of gritstone brought to the site from the nearest outcrops at least 10 miles away at Cayton. In the north-east corner of Rudston churchyard is a large stone cist removed from a local round barrow.

STANWICK, *Stanwick-St-John, North Yorkshire. NGR: NZ 180115*
Probably a major stronghold of the Brigantes tribe who occupied much of what is now Yorkshire at the time of the Roman Conquest, this massive enclosure covering nearly 304ha straddles the valley of Mary Wild Beck. Excavations by Sir Mortimer Wheeler in 1951—2 revealed much about the site, which clearly developed in several stages.

In the early 1st century AD, a small defended enclosure of about 6.8ha was established in the area now called the Tofts. The single rampart can still be seen to the south of the church as a grass-covered bank and ditch. This fort was enlarged shortly afterwards by demolishing the northern rampart and expanding the site north of Mary Wild Beck. This second enclosure was again bounded by a single rampart, and a stretch on the north-west side was restored for display following its excavation. It can still be seen today (signposted), and provides a very vivid impression of just how well the site was originally defended.

In the final phase of remodelling, probably about AD70, a large annexe of some 242.7ha was added to the south of the existing enclosure. Much of this new area, again bounded by a single rampart, may have been used to provide protection for herds of animals.

The Brigantes, under their leader Venutius, were finally subjugated by the Roman army sometime between AD71 and AD74. Stanwick was stormed, the defences slighted, and thereafter intensive occupation of the site ended.
ENGLISH HERITAGE

THORNBOROUGH HENGES, *near Ripon, North Yorkshire. NGR: SE 285795*
Spread out along the valley floor of the River Ure, about ½ mile north-east of the river, are three large, round, late Neolithic henge monuments. They lie at intervals of just over ½ mile on a single axis running in a direction roughly north-west to south-east.

All three are about 245m in diameter and of similar design. Nearly circular in plan, they all have two opposing entrances to the north-west and south-east. The massive banks originally stood about 9.1m high, but

unlike most henges these had ditches on both sides of their banks. These ditches, now mostly silted up, were separated from the banks by a berm 12m wide. The most completely preserved of the three is the northern circle which today is covered in trees.

Thornborough's trio (one densely covered in trees) of circular henges

Excavations in 1952 revealed that the banks of these henges had been covered in gypsum crystals, perhaps to make them look white like the henges of Wessex. The central henge was built over the top of a cursus which extends north-eastwards from the site for nearly a mile. Its ditches had silted up before the henge was built and nothing of the cursus is now visible on the ground.

Little is known of the activities that took place inside these henges, but their alignment and the fact that their entrances lie on a common axis suggest that together they served as a large and important ceremonial centre.

VICTORIA CAVE, *Settle,*
North Yorkshire. NGR: SD 838650

Set in limestone cliffs overlooking the Ribble Valley, this large cave contains three chambers which can still be entered through its gaping westward-facing mouth. Inviting as a refuge and for its panoramic views, the site was intermittently occupied by animals and people since the later phases of the last Ice Age.

During the late Devensian period the cave was the den of a pack of hyaena, and with their bones were the remains of hippopotamus, woolly rhinoceros and elephant. Later, in late upper Palaeolithic times, a group of hunters lived in the cave for a while, leaving behind a variety of tools and weapons. Among the debris were two antler points, one of which is decorated with incised wavy lines.

Traces of Mesolithic activity at the site in the form of a distinctive barbed harpoon point have been found. There was also evidence of occupation in Roman times.

YEAVERING BELL, *near Kirknewton,*
Northumberland. NGR: NT 928293

Perched on the very northern edge of the Cheviot Hills at a height of 350m above sea level, this great hillfort overlooks the valley of the River Glen to the north, and is the largest site of its kind in Northumberland.

The defences comprise a single stout wall enclosing about 5.2ha. The wall was originally 3m to 3.6m thick and 2.4m high. There are entrances on the north, south and east sides, all now represented by gaps in the wall, and two small annexes can still be seen.

Inside the fort are over 130 house platforms ranging from 5.4m to 9.1m in

Top and above: *Yeavering Bell's lofty defences look down on to peaceful Northumberland farming country*

diameter, today visible as scoops cut into the hillside. Most seem to have been intended for round buildings, although one or two are rectangular in plan. Around the easternmost of the two summits within the fort are traces of a circular ditch or palisade. Little is known about this feature, but it may relate to an early (possibly pre-hillfort) period of occupation on the site. A Bronze Age round barrow lies within the palisade.

The construction of the fort has not been accurately dated, but it probably took place during the later Iron Age, with occupation continuing well into the Roman period.

SCOTLAND

*T*he mountainous highlands of Scotland were generally avoided by prehistoric communities, but around the fringes of the uplands, along the coast and in the main river valleys, settlement was just as intensive as in other parts of Britain.

Neolithic and Bronze Age monuments are well represented in the agriculturally rich areas of the south-west, the Central Lowlands and eastern Scotland. Comparable monuments also occur widely on the islands off the west coast, in Orkney and in Shetland. Among the monuments of this period which are peculiar to Scotland are the developed passage graves, Clava Cairns and recumbent stone circles.

In Iron Age times the north of Scotland was occupied by small communities living in distinctive kinds of fortified homesteads, brochs and duns found only in this area, while in the Borders and Southern Uplands larger hillforts dating from later prehistoric times are fairly numerous.

Prehistory essentially continued well into the 1st millennium AD throughout Scotland because, despite advances north of Hadrian's Wall in the late 1st, middle 2nd and early 3rd centuries AD, the Roman army never won control of northern Britain.

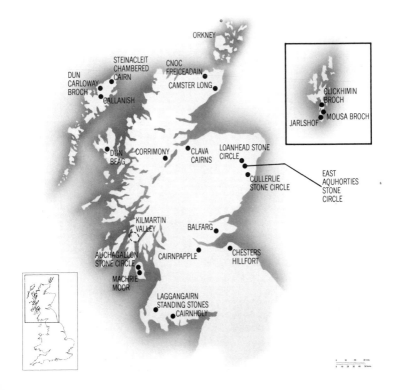

AUCHAGALLON STONE CIRCLE,

Arran, Strathclyde. NGR: NR 893346
Overlooking Machrie Bay, this circle of
15 standing stones surrounds a round
cairn. The circle measures about 14.9m
in diameter. About 2 miles to the south
is the group of circles and burial
monuments on Machrie Moor (page 113).
*HISTORIC BUILDINGS AND
MONUMENTS*

BALFARG, *Glenrothes, Fife.*

Centred on NGR: NO 285030
Beside the main A92(T) to the north-east
of Glenrothes is an important group of
late Neolithic ceremonial monuments
which have been carefully restored.

West of the road is **Balfarg Henge**
[NGR: NO 283031], excavated in 1977—8
and now put down to grass with posts
to mark some of the uprights that once
stood inside the monument. The main
ditch is horseshoe shaped, about 76m
across, and open on the south-west side.
No trace of a bank remains.

Two phases of construction were
recognised. In the first, dating to about
3200BC, there were six roughly

concentric rings of wooden posts inside
the henge. The second ring in was the
most substantial, and this is the one
now marked out on the ground.
Whether all six rings were standing at
the same time is uncertain.

In the second phase, probably
about 2800BC, the wooden posts were
replaced by two rings of upright stones.
The outer ring contained 24 stones, the
inner ring 16. The entrance to the ring
was marked by a pair of stones on each
side, and the remains of these, together
with an outlier positioned just outside
the entrance, can still be seen. The
centre of the monument was found to
contain a burial accompanied by a
beaker pot and a flint knife.

East of the road is the **Balbirne
Stone Circle** *[NGR: NO 285029]*, re-
erected on its present site following the
complete excavation of the original
structure during the widening of the
A92(T) in 1971. The circle, constructed in
late Neolithic times, had a maximum
diameter of about 15m and comprised 10
large upright stones. In the centre was a
rectangular area defined by stone slabs.

The cist and the tallest of the stones at Balbirne

Sometime later, four stone-lined cists containing burials were constructed within the circle. A burial accompanied by a beaker pot was deposited in an unlined pit. All these burials were then covered with a mound of stones about 1m high. Finally, at least 16 cremations were either inserted into the top of the mound or scattered over it.

CAIRNHOLY, *near Creetown, Dumfries and Galloway. NGR: NX 518541*
This pair of middle Neolithic long barrows lie on gently sloping ground above the steep-sided valley of the Kirkdale Burn. The southernmost barrow, partly restored, is the most impressive and belongs to the Clyde-Carlingford tradition of long barrow building. The mound is over 42.6m long by 10m wide. It is orientated roughly east to west with a chamber and forecourt at the east end.

Originally the cairn was edged with boulders but these have mostly disappeared. The forecourt is dominated by a façade of eight upright slabs, the two in the centre forming a narrow entrance to the chamber. Traces of fires were found in the forecourt, presumably relics of the rituals that took place there. The prostrate stone in the forecourt is the blocking stone that once acted as a door for the chamber.

The chamber itself is rectangular in plan, constructed of large upright slabs, the gaps between the slabs being filled with dry-stone walling. It is divided into two portions by a large stone slab. Nothing remains of the roof. The chamber was found to contain some cremated bone.

The northern cairn is slightly smaller, but of similar design.
HISTORIC BUILDINGS AND MONUMENTS

CAIRNPAPPLE HILL*, *near Bathgate, Lothian. NGR: NS 987717*
At a height of over 300m above sea level, the succession of Neolithic and early Bronze Age ceremonial monuments constructed on this hilltop commanded exceptional views. The earliest use of the hill was as a cremation cemetery about 3000BC. Seven pits arranged in an arc received the burials, one of them accompanied by a bone pin.

The grave at Cairnpapple Hill

About 2500BC a henge with two entrances was constructed. Inside was an oval setting of 24 upright stones with a maximum diameter of 35m. Two graves containing beaker pots were found in the henge; one has been reconstructed for display.

Several centuries later the henge was deliberately destroyed and a round barrow some 15m in diameter constructed in its place. At the centre was a cist containing a single burial accompanied by a food vessel. The barrow was later enlarged and two cremations in collared urns added. Four further burials were made during Iron Age times.
HISTORIC BUILDINGS AND MONUMENTS (see page 116)

CALLANISH, *Lewis, Western Isles.*
NGR: NB 213330
The quality and remoteness of this late Neolithic monument overlooking Loch Roag at Callanish make this site especially attractive.

Callanish's numerous standing stones

In the centre of the monument is a stone pillar over 4.5m high. Around it is a ring of 13 upright stones constructed as a flattened circle with a maximum diameter of 11.2m. Within the circle, on the east side, is a small passage grave set in a round mound that includes the central pillar and two stones of the circle in its kerb. This tomb was probably added to the circle rather than vice-versa.

Radiating from the central circle are five rows of upright stones. To the north-east are two roughly parallel lines forming an avenue 8.2m wide and over 82m long. To the south a single line of five stones extends for a distance of 27.5m, and on the east and west sides shorter lines of four stones run for a distance of 15.2m and 12.1m respectively. Various astronomical alignments have been claimed for these rows, but few of them are convincing.

HISTORIC BUILDINGS AND MONUMENTS

CAMSTER LONG, *near Watten,*
Highland. NGR: ND 260440
Two Neolithic tombs, both partly restored, can be seen at Camster beside the minor road that runs northwards from Lybster to Watten. The larger of the two, Camster Long, developed in two stages. The earliest construction was the simple passage grave which is now visible towards the centre of the long mound. The central chamber of this monument is approached from the south-east along a narrow passage. Once inside notice how it is divided into three compartments by stone slabs.

In the second stage, the tomb was remodelled and a massive wedge-shaped mound over 60m long was constructed over the top of the earlier structure. A forecourt flanked by two horns can be

Camster Long's huge, rocky mound

seen at each end, and a polygonal chamber approached by a long passage from the south-east lies near the wider, higher end of the mound. The mound has a stepped profile.

The nearby site of **Camster Round** is more modest in scale, about 18m in diameter, 3.6m high, and contains a chamber of similar plan and orientation to the early chamber at Camster Long. The remains of at least six people were found in the chamber.

HISTORIC BUILDINGS AND MONUMENTS

CHESTERS HILLFORT, *near Drem, Lothian. NGR: NT 507782*

Set amid rolling countryside at about 122m above sea level, the compact size and delightfully rounded ramparts of this Iron Age hillfort make it one of the best-preserved examples of its type in south-eastern Scotland.

The inner enclosure is oval in plan, about 116m by 46m, bounded all round by a strong rampart which now survives as a bank 18m wide and 2m high. There is an entrance to the east-south-east, and the gap on the west side may possibly be original.

A second line of ramparts, slightly less substantial than the first, is 13.7m wide and 1.5m high. Traces of a further four banks beyond these can also be seen. Rather surprisingly, this hillfort stands below a fairly steep escarpment.

Among the many other hillforts in south-east Scotland, **Traprain Law** *[NGR: NT 581746]* and **Eildon Hill** *[NGR: NT 555328]* are two which are particularly worth visiting.
HISTORIC BUILDINGS AND MONUMENTS

CLAVA CAIRNS, *Inverness, Highland. NGR: NH 756445*

The late Neolithic tombs at Clava, partly restored, stand in a line on a north-east to south-west axis. All three are round in plan and each is surrounded by a stone circle.

The central tomb is of the ring-cairn type. Constructed of massive boulders edged with a kerb of even larger stones, the cairn was heaped up to a height of about 1.2m. The central area is edged by flat stones, and during excavation in 1857 was found to contain cremated human bone.

The two outer tombs are typical of the type of monuments generally known as Clava Cairns, and as such form part of a widespread late Neolithic tradition of tomb-building in northern and western Britain which also includes the entrance graves of West Penwith (page 33) and the Scilly Isles (see Bant's Cairn, page 24).

Both the outer tombs at Clava have circular cairns edged with large boulders. In the centre of each is a circular chamber approached by a passage from the south-west, an axis that may be significant as it coincides with the midwinter sunset. Large upright stones form the walls of the chambers and passages, while the roofs were originally corbelled. Human bone, some cremated, has been found in both of the chambers.
HISTORIC BUILDINGS AND MONUMENTS

The south-western cairn and circle at Clava

CLICKHIMIN BROCH, *Shetland.*
NGR: HU 465408

Now set on a promontory in Loch Clickhimin, in prehistoric times this site was on an island. The earliest visible remains are the walls of a small undefended farmstead dating to the 8th or 9th century BC.

In the 5th or 6th century BC, the farmstead was replaced by a fort bounded by a stout dry-stone wall. As visible today, this wall has been partly reconstructed. There was a single entrance to the south-east, and just outside the gate was a landing stage. Inside the fort were several timber buildings and, near the centre, a large blockhouse originally three stories high.

In late Iron Age times a broch was constructed within the fort. This circular tower was 19.8m in diameter and originally 12m to 15m high; just over 5m of it remain. The central courtyard was 10m in diameter and there were at least two rooms in the walls. The broch was occupied well into the first millennium AD. In post-Roman times the need for defence seems to have been less and a

Settlement spanned many centuries at Clickhimin Broch. Appearances are deceptive: although now located on a promontory, this was originally an island site

wheelhouse, occupied until the 9th century AD, was constructed in the centre of the broch.
HISTORIC BUILDINGS AND MONUMENTS

CNOC FREICEADAIN, *near Thurso, Highland. NGR: ND 012654*

This pair of long barrows lie about 125m apart and are positioned at right-angles to one another.

Cnoc Freiceadain is about 67m long, 16m wide, and orientated south-west to north-east. Horns can be seen at both ends of the mound, although those at the south-western end are less clear. Various stones projecting through the robbed cairn may indicate the positions of chambers. At the south-western end the cairn appears to rise into a round mound with a flat top.

Na Tri Shean, which commands a magnificent view over Caithness and Orkney, is about 71.6m long, 21.3m wide, and orientated south-east to north-west. Horns can be clearly seen at both ends, and in profile the cairn rises at either end into distinct circular mounds. A few slabs indicating the possible position of chambers can be seen in the mound.
HISTORIC BUILDINGS AND MONUMENTS

CORRIMONY, *Glen Urquhart,*
Highland. NGR: NH 383303
This passage grave constructed in the
Clava Cairn tradition lies on the level
flood plain of the River Enrick.
Excavated in 1952, and since partly
restored, the mound is about 14m in
diameter and consists of water-worn
boulders and pebbles. A kerb surrounds
the cairn, larger and longer slabs being
used around the entrance on the south-
west side, presumably to give it a more
imposing appearance.

About 3.9m beyond the kerb is a
circle of 11 standing stones. The south-
western axis of the passage and chamber
here, as at other passage graves in the
Clava tradition, suggests some interest
in the midwinter sunset.
HISTORIC BUILDINGS AND
MONUMENTS

In the centre of the cairn is a
circular chamber, 3.6m in diameter,
approached by a narrow passage, 7m
long, from the south-west. The walls of
both passage and chamber are formed of
large orthostats. A layer of water-worn
pebbles covered the floor of the
chamber, sealing a sandy surface bearing
faint traces of a crouched body. Since
excavation, the chamber and passage
have been closed off for safety reasons.

The entrance to the passage grave at Corrimony

CULLERLIE STONE CIRCLE, *near*
Peterculter, Grampian. NGR: NJ 785043
This small stone circle comprises eight
rather squat undressed boulders set at
roughly equal intervals on the
circumference of an almost perfect circle
with a diameter of 9.7m. Excavated in
1934, the site is now partly restored.

Cairns within the circle at Cullerlie

Within the circle are eight small
ring cairns. The largest cairn lies almost
in the centre, the others being in the
space between the central cairn and the
ring of stones. Each cairn is edged with
a kerb of boulders.

Traces of a burnt floor — resulting
from the lighting of many fires — were
discovered below the cairns. Fire pits in
which human remains had been
cremated were also found. Abundant
traces of willow charcoal were found
within the circle, oak charcoal was found
in five of the inner cairns, and hazel
charcoal in the westernmost cairn.
Cremated human bone was also found
around and within the cairns.
HISTORIC BUILDINGS AND
MONUMENTS

DUN BEAG, *Struan, Bracadale, Skye, Highland. NGR: NG 339386*
Set on a rocky knoll overlooking the coast road, this broch was excavated in 1915. The wall is up to 4.2m thick, and surrounds an inner courtyard some 10.6m in diameter. The entrance, with substantial door-checks, is on the east, and as you go into the site notice the door to a stairway leading up through the wall to the left. On the right of the door is a small room opening into the wall from the inner court, and almost opposite the entrance is a raised door to a gallery inside the wall.

About a 250m to the north is **Dun Mor** *[NGR: NG 339390]*, a small Iron Age fort.

Although ruined, the construction techniques employed at Dun Carloway are plain to see

The remains of the moorland broch, Dun Beag

DUN CARLOWAY BROCH,

near Carloway, Lewis, Western Isles. NGR: NB 189412
Set on a rocky knoll, this Iron Age broch shows many characteristic features of its type. The slightly tapering solid walls of the central tower, surviving to a height of about 10m, can be clearly seen. The walls are about 3.3m thick, and the central courtyard is 7.6m in diameter.

The entrance passage, which faces north-west, retains its fittings and guard cell in good condition. There are four doors from the central courtyard to cells and galleries within the wall. In 1861, four upper galleries and part of a fifth were preserved, but, sadly, most of this has now gone.

The internal structure of the broch wall is clearly visible at this site. Constructed with two skins bonded together by cross-slabs, the centre of the wall was used for chambers and stairs. One of the chambers entered at ground level gives access to a flight of stairs.

About 2.1m above ground level is a scarcement or ledge. This supported a wooden gallery, but whether it extended right across the inside of the broch like a floor or was simply a platform around the edge is not clear. Indeed, it has never been satisfactorily resolved whether or not any of the brochs were roofed. If they were not, then any fire which started at ground level in the courtyard would turn the tower into a blast furnace. As fortified dwellings, most brochs were home to between 30 and 50 individuals.
HISTORIC BUILDINGS AND MONUMENTS

EAST AQUHORTIES STONE CIRCLE *Inverurie, Grampian.*
NGR: NJ 733208

Although never excavated, this stone circle is a splendid example of what are known as recumbent stone circles. Such circles are distinctive because they have a large prostrate stone set between two uprights or 'flankers', usually in the south-west sector of the circle. Recumbent stone circles are peculiar to north-east Scotland, although whether they were used any differently from stone circles elsewhere is not known.

Eleven upright stones stand on the circumference of this circle, which has a diameter of about 19.8m. Two flank the recumbent stone on the south-west side, and there are two additional stones inside the circle next to the recumbent stone. The stones are graded in height so that the tallest are nearest to the recumbent stone. Most of the stones are local in origin, but the large recumbent slab may have been brought to the site from some distance away.

The near-circular form of the ring and its neat, compact, recumbent setting suggest that it was constructed around approximately 2500BC.
HISTORIC BUILDINGS AND MONUMENTS

JARLSHOF*, *Shetland.*
NGR: HU 397096

This site was brought to light by a great storm in 1897, and has since been excavated and restored for display. Like Clickhimin (page 106), it has a long and complicated history spanning over 1,000 years, and provides important evidence of the prehistory and early history of the far north of Scotland.

The earliest visible features are the stone foundations of unenclosed houses of a small, late Bronze Age village, partly overlain by slightly larger houses dating to the early Iron Age. Finds from these buildings include agricultural implements and evidence of metalworking. In the third main phase a broch was constructed, probably in the early 1st century AD. About half of the central tower survives, enough to show that it had a solid base, an overall diameter of 19.5m and walls some 5.4m thick. Around the central tower was a second courtyard which was bounded by a stout wall.

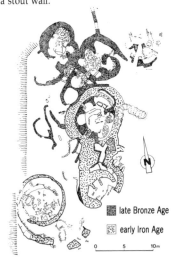

late Bronze Age

early Iron Age

0   5   10m

Plan of the early unfortified villages at Jarlshof (after Hamilton 1956)

Occupation continued into the 1st millennium AD with several further phases represented by remains of a wheelhouse of late Roman date, a Viking village, a hamlet of 11th to 13th century AD date, a medieval farm, and finally a post-medieval laird's house christened 'Jarlshof' by Sir Walter Scott.
HISTORIC BUILDINGS AND MONUMENTS (see page 116)

KILMARTIN VALLEY, *Strathclyde*

The area between Kilmartin and Lochgilphead is one of the richest archaeological zones in western Scotland. All along the valley are natural boulders bearing incised decoration and cup-and-ring marks.

At **Achnabreck** *[NGR: NR 856906]* two large areas of rock are covered in elaborate pecked designs including double spirals. To the west at **Cairnbaan** *[NGR: NR 838910]* are two groups of carving, both showing cup-marks, cup-and-ring marks and some grooves. To the north is **Kilmichael Glassary** *[NGR: NR 858935]*, a large slab set into the earth and covered in cup-marks, cup-and-ring marks and keyhole figures. Nearby is the early medieval fort of **Dunadd** *[NGR: NR 837936]*.

Continuing further north there are more incised stones at **Buluachraig** *[NGR: NR 831970]*, where a glaciated rock surface has many well-preserved cup-and-ring marks. Finally, at **Ballygowan Rocks** *[NGR: NR 820974]*, the designs include radial grooves, ovals and one horseshoe figure.

Early forms of decorative art on Ballygowan Rocks

All these decorated rocks are thought to be of Bronze Age date, and certainly the period of 2500BC to 1000BC seems to have been a time of widespread activity in the area to judge from the other monuments.

The cist surrounded by the incomplete Temple Wood Stone Circle

The **Temple Wood Stone Circle** *[NGR: NR 826979]* originally comprised 20 stones set on a low bank 12.1m in diameter. Only 13 now remain, but the bank can be seen. At the centre of the circle is a stone cist measuring 1.5m by 0.9m, with a low setting of slabs around it. Traces of cremated bone were found in it. One slab of a pair originally marking the entrance survives on the south-east side. A pecked spiral design has recently been discovered on one of the upright stones.

To the south are the five **Nether Largie Standing Stones** *[NGR: NR 828976]*. These comprise two pairs and a single stone in a line running north-east to south-west. The central stone bears cup-marks, and it has been suggested that the stones mark significant astronomical alignments. Two such alignments have been proposed. In the first the two stones at the south end point north-west to the Temple Wood Circle and thence away to a notch in the hill beyond, which marks the most northerly setting of the moon. The second alignment involves looking south-westwards along the row to Bellanoch Hill (now there are trees in the way) which marks the extreme southerly setting of the moon.

Other standing stones in the area include the **Ballymeanock Standing Stones** *[NGR: NR 833964]*. This group comprises six uprights, the tallest over 4.2m high, arranged in an unusual formation of two lines, one containing four stones, the other two stones. Two of the stones in the longer line bear cup-and-ring marks, as does a fallen outlier north-west of the pair. About 100m south-west of the stones are the remains of a denuded henge monument. Other standing stones can be seen west of **Bridgend** *[NGR: NR 846927]* on the south side of the River Add.

The group of round barrows forming the **Nether Largie Barrow Cemetery** dominates the evidence for burial monuments in the area. There are five cairns in all, arranged in a line roughly north to south. At the south end is the **Ri Cruin Cairn** *[NGR: NR 825972]*, now rather denuded but at one time containing three cists. One of the slabs in the south cist carried carvings of bronze axeheads.

Next in line is **Nether Largie South** *[NGR: NR 829980]*, the oldest barrow in the cemetery. When excavated in 1864 it

The entrance to Nether Largie South

The interior, Nether Largie South

was found to contain cremations of early Neolithic date in a central chamber. Beaker burials were later inserted into the cairn.

Nether Largie Middle *[NGR: NR 830983]* was excavated in 1929 and proved to be circular, about 30m in diameter, and originally edged with a boulder kerb. It contained two cists, the one in the north-west part of the mound having side stones jointed together as if they were wood. Both cists were empty when opened.

Nether Largie North *[NGR: NR 831984]* is 21.3m in diameter and 2.7m high. It is set within a rubble bank. The stones in the central cist had a number of carvings on them, thought to depict Bronze Age metal axes.

Finally, the northernmost barrow is the **Glebe Cairn** *[NGR: NR 833989]*, another round mound about 33.2m in diameter. Explored in 1864, it was found to have a central cist in which was a single inhumation burial accompanied by a food vessel. A second cist to the south-west also contained a food vessel, together with a jet necklace.

LAGGANGAIRN STANDING
STONES, *Kilgallioch, Dumfries and Galloway. NGR: NX 222717*
Overlooking the Ring Burn, these two standing stones may be the last remnants of a Bronze Age stone circle. The northern stone is 2m high, the other 1.6m high. Both have Latin crosses carved on their west faces. Local tradition records that several more stones once existed at the site, and that the square pillar to the east of the surviving pair marks the grave of a farmer who removed some of the stones.
HISTORIC BUILDINGS AND MONUMENTS

LOANHEAD STONE CIRCLE,
Daviot, Grampian. NGR: NJ 748288
Excavated in 1934, and since partly restored, this recumbent stone circle is one of the best examples of its type. Standing near the summit of a gentle hill, nine stones lie on the circumference of the circle which is about 20.5m in diameter. The stones are graded in height with the focus on the recumbent slab which lies to the south-west.

Inside the circle is a low cairn of stones edged by a kerb of small boulders. At the centre of the cairn is an open area some 3.6m in diameter. Excavations revealed a rectangular wooden structure at the centre of the circle, possibly pre-dating the construction of the cairn. Skull fragments of children were found in this central area.

To the south-east of the main circle was an oval arrangement of stones with its main axis aligned on the midwinter sunrise. There are also five outlying stones to the west and south-east of the circle. Beaker pottery was found at the site, suggesting that the circle was constructed about 2400BC. Sometime later, small cairns of stones were piled up around the circle's main uprights, one covering a cist which contained a small pot of middle Bronze Age date.

As at all recumbent stone circles, the prostrate recumbent slab was obviously the focus of attention. Quartz pebbles lay around the recumbent stone. Careful observations have shown that when viewed from the centre of the circle, the southern moon at its extreme rising or setting appears to roll along the top of the stone, a phenomenon neatly framed by the flankers.
HISTORIC BUILDINGS AND MONUMENTS

The recumbent slab at Loanhead served as the focus of the site

MACHRIE MOOR, *Arran, Strathclyde.*
NGR: NR 912324

This low-lying expanse of moorland on the western side of Arran seems to have been a major centre for early Bronze Age ritual and ceremonial activity.

At the focus is a double stone circle known as **Fingal's Cauldron Seat.** The inner ring of eight granite boulders forms an almost perfect circle about 12.1m in diameter. The outer circle, also of granite boulders, is egg shaped. A ruined cist was found at the centre of the inner circle, but it was empty. Legend records that the giant Fingal once tied his dog Bran to one of the stones in the outer circle (the one with the hole in) while he cooked himself a meal in the inner circle.

From Fingal's Cauldron Seat it is possible to see most of the other six stone circles and various standing stones that lie scattered over the moor. Most date to between 1800BC and 1600BC, a time before the formation of the blanket bog which now covers most of the moor.

MOUSA BROCH, *Shetland.*
NGR: HU 457236

Set on the tiny island of Mousa to the east of mainland Shetland, this great stone tower is built straight on to the rock overlooking Mousa Sound. Undoubtedly the best-preserved broch in Scotland, it still stands over 12m high and is constructed of dry-stone walling of the very highest standard.

The broch tower has an external diameter of 15.2m at the base, but tapers inwards slightly towards the top. To withstand the gales and high winds that blow in from the North Sea the wall is over 6m thick.

Opening off the central courtyard are three large corbelled cells with low doorways. There are three wall-cupboards in the side of the inner court. Two ledges representing supports for upper floors or galleries can be seen. The upper ledge may have supported the roof. The inner wall-face also contains sets of openings or voids which may have been to allow light into the galleries contained within the walls.

Mousa Broch, remote and well preserved

A stair rises clockwise inside the wall allowing access to six galleries. It is unlikely that these galleries were ever lived in, although they could have been used for storage. Judging from its superior design and craftsmanship, this broch was probably constructed fairly late in the tradition of broch building.
HISTORIC BUILDINGS AND MONUMENTS

ORKNEY

Once described as an archaeological wonderland, the Orkneys preserve a bewildering range of monuments, many of them of Neolithic date.

The tomb at **Isbister,** *South Ronaldsay [NGR: ND 470845]*, now appears as an oval-shaped mound about 41m long by 15.2m wide. Excavations have revealed a single chamber near the centre of the mound, approached by a passage from the north-east. The chamber is rectangular in plan with three side cells leading off it. The remains of at least 341 individuals were found here, probably representing the dead of a small farming community over the period 3200BC to 2400BC. Among the human burials there were bones of white-tailed eagles — perhaps the totem of the community.

On Rousay, the tomb of **Mid Howe** *[NGR: HY 372306]* is now displayed inside a specially constructed building. Again of middle to late Neolithic date, this is perhaps the finest example of a type of tomb known as a stalled-cairn. The mound is roughly rectangular, 32m long by 12.8m wide. The central chamber measures 23.1m long by 2.1m wide, and was approached through a short passage from the south-east. It is divided into 12 compartments by pairs of upright stones projecting from the walls. Low shelves have been inserted in seven of the compartments, and it was on these shelves that the bones of 25 individuals were discovered.

In central Mainland is the **Unstan Chambered Cairn** *[NGR: HY 283117]*, another stalled-cairn, but of more modest proportions than Mid Howe. The mound is circular, with a short passage opening from the south-east side to provide access to the chamber. The chamber is rectangular, about 6m long by 1.8m wide. It is divided into five compartments by pairs of projecting stones. A small side cell opens westwards from the main chamber.

Many other tombs can be seen on Orkney, but perhaps the most impressive is **Maeshowe*** *[NGR: HY 318128]* in central Mainland (see page 116). The great domed mound, now covered in rough grass, is well over 7m high and 35m in diameter. It is composed of soil and rock, and is surrounded by a partly silted-up ditch over 18m wide.

Under the centre of the mound, approached via a long, narrow passage from the south-west, is a square-shaped chamber off which three side cells radiate. The passage is only 1.3m high and you have to stoop as you go into the tomb, but the central chamber is over 3.6m high and amazingly roomy. Both passage and chamber are constructed of local stone put together with great skill. There are no certain prehistoric finds from the site, although radiocarbon dates suggest that construction began about 2700BC. In the 12th century AD the tomb was visited by Norsemen who carved a series of runic inscriptions inside the chamber. A mystical spirit known as 'Hogboy' is said to act as the tomb's guardian.

Domestic fixtures and fittings, late Neolithic style, at Skara Brae

Within the walls of another dwelling at Skara Brae

Other ceremonial sites on Orkney include henges. At the **Ring of Brogar** [NGR: HY 294134], magnificently placed between the Loch of Harry and the Loch of Stenness, a circular ditch about 112m in diameter, 9.1m wide and 1.8m deep defines the perimeter of the henge. There are entrances to the north-west and south-east, but no traces of an external bank. Inside, about 3m from the inner lip of the ditch, was a stone circle originally containing some 60 stones. Only 27 remain standing, mostly large flat slabs between 1.5m and 4.5m tall.

To the south-east is a second henge, the **Stones of Stenness** [NGR: HY 306126]. Little now remains of the bank and ditch of this site which was originally 61m in diameter, but a single entrance lies to the north. Four massive stones remain of the ring of 13 slabs that once stood inside the monument. Cists and pits containing burials have been found in the henge, and radiocarbon dates suggest that it was constructed about 2900BC.

Settlements of late Neolithic date are also known, of which the most notable is **Skara Brae*** [NGR: HY 231188] on the exposed west coast of Mainland Orkney overlooking the wild Atlantic Ocean (see page 116). In its main phase, about 2900BC, this settlement comprised up to eight roughly square houses connected together by a series of passages. Each house was equipped with a central hearth and a number of sleeping places. Some houses had other furniture and items made out of stone (eg shelves, dressers and fish tanks). The roofs of the houses are now missing, but the walls still stand to shoulder height.

Evidence of Iron Age occupation is also abundant on Orkney, and one of the most impressive sites is the **Broch of Gurness*** (see page 116) [NGR: HY 383268]. Here the central tower lies within a group of buildings and defences, some contemporary with the broch but many of them later.

STEINACLEIT CHAMBERED CAIRN, Lewis, Western Isles.
NGR: NB 396540

This rather ruinous cairn, probably of late Neolithic or Bronze Age date, is about 16.4m in diameter and edged with a kerb of large stone blocks. Around the north part of the cairn the wall is continuous and includes large stones set horizontally between natural boulders.

The cairn itself is built of loose stones, banked up near the edge to a height of about 1m. The centre is dished, and there are several large stones which appear to belong to a structure, perhaps a chamber. The most notable is an upright on the west side which projects nearly 1.2m.

HISTORIC BUILDINGS AND MONUMENTS

SITES WITH RESTRICTED OPENING

Most prehistoric monuments can be visited at any reasonable time, but some sites, mostly those under private management or in the charge of a custodian, have restricted opening hours. To avoid disappointment it is advisable to check opening times in advance, especially if you are making a long journey.

In the West Country:

Avebury Museum, *Avebury, nr Marlborough, Wiltshire SN8 1RF. (Tel. 06723-250)*

Chysauster Ancient Village, *nr Gulval, Cornwall (Tel. 0736-61889)*

Gough's Cave, *Cheddar, Somerset BS27 3QF. (Tel. 0934-742343)*

Somerset Levels Museum, *Willows Garden Centre, Shapwick Road, Westhay, Glastonbury, Somerset. (Tel. 04586-257)*

Stanton Drew, *Stanton Drew, Avon. (English Heritage area office for details: Tel. 0272-734472 extn 205)*

Stonehenge, *Wiltshire. (English Heritage area office for details: Tel. 0272-734472 extn 205)*

Wookey Hole, *Wells, Somerset BA5 1BB. (Tel. 0749-72243)*

In South and South-East England:

Butser Hill Experimental Iron Age Farm, *Queen Elizabeth Country Park, nr Petersfield, Hampshire. (Tel. 0705-598838)*

Chestnuts Long Barrow, *'Rose Alba', Park Road, Addington, Kent.*

High Rocks, *High Rocks Hotel, High Rocks Lane, Tunbridge Wells, Kent.*

In Wales:

Castellhenllys Excavation, *Eglwyswrw, Dyfed. (Tel. 023979-319)*

In Central England and East Anglia:

Creswell Crags Visitor Centre, *off Crags Road, Welbeck, Worksop, Nottinghamshire. (Tel. 0909-720378)*

Flag Fen Excavations, *4th Drove, Fengate, Peterborough, Cambridgeshire. (Tel. 0733-313414)*

Grimes Graves, *nr Thetford, Norfolk. (Tel. 0842-810656)*

In Scotland:

For the Scottish sites listed below, please contact Historic Buildings and Monuments for details: Tel. 031-244 3085.

Broch of Gurness, *Orkney*

Cairnpapple Hill, *Central*

Jarlshof, *Shetland*

Maeshowe, *Orkney*

Skara Brae, *Orkney*

MUSEUMS TO VISIT

Very few prehistoric sites in Britain are provided with museums or display centres where finds and explanatory material can be seen. This is a shame, but is in part compensated for by the fact that all three national museums in Britain, and most county, district and borough museums, display prehistoric material. The following are particularly worth visiting:

In the West Country:

Bristol City Museum and Art Gallery, *Queen's Road, Clifton, Bristol BS8 1RL. (Tel. 0272-299771)*

Corinium Museum, *Park Street, Cirencester GL7 2BX. (Tel. 0285-5611)*

Dorset County Museum, *High West Street, Dorchester DT1 1XA. (Tel. 0305-62735)*

Royal Albert Memorial Museum, *Queen Street, Exeter EX4 3RX. (Tel. 0392-265858)*

Salisbury and South Wiltshire Museum, *The Close. Salisbury SP1 2EN. (Tel. 0722-332151)*

Wiltshire Archaeological and Natural History Society Museum, *Long Street, Devizes SN10 1NS. (Tel. 0380-77369)*

In South and South-East England:

Ashmolean Museum, *Beaumont Street, Oxford OX1 2PH. (Tel. 0865-278000)*
British Museum, *Great Russell Street, London WC1B 3DG. (Tel. 01-636 1555)*
Museum of the Iron Age, *Church Street, Andover SP10 1DP. (Tel. 0264-66283)*
Oxfordshire County Museum, *Fletcher's House, Woodstock OX7 1SP. (Tel. 0993-811456)*

In Wales:

Museum of Welsh Antiquities, *Ffordd Gwynedd, Bangor LL57 1DT. (Tel. 0248-353368)*
National Museum of Wales, *Cathays Park, Cardiff CF1 3NP. (Tel. 0222-397951)*
Tenby Museum, *Castle Hill, Tenby SA70 7BP. (Tel. 0834-2809)*

In Central England and East Anglia:

Birmingham Museum and Art Gallery, *Chamberlain Square, Birmingham B3 3DH. (Tel. 021-235 3890)*
The Castle Museum, *The Castle, Norwich NR1 3JU. (Tel. 0603-611277)*
University Museum of Archaeology and Anthropology, *Downing Street, Cambridge CB2 3DZ. (Tel. 0223-333510)*

In the North Country:

Doncaster Museum and Art Gallery, *Chequer Street, Doncaster DN1 2AE. (Tel. 0302-734287)*
Merseyside County Museum, *William Brown Street, Liverpool L3 8EN. (Tel. 051-207 0001)*
Sheffield City Museum, *Weston Park, Sheffield S10 2TP. (Tel. 0742-768588)*
Yorkshire Museum, *Museum Gardens, York YO1 2DR. (Tel. 0904-629745)*

In Scotland:

Central Museum and Art Gallery, *Albert Square, Dundee DD1 1DA. (Tel. 0382-23141)*
City of Glasgow Museum and Art Gallery, *Kelvingrove, Glasgow G3 8AG. (Tel. 041-357 3929)*
Royal Museum of Scotland, *Queen Street, Edinburgh EH2 1JD. (Tel. 031-557 3550)*

FURTHER READING

Recent general accounts of Britain before the Romans include *Prehistoric Britain* by **Timothy Darvill** (Batsford, 1987) and *An Introduction to British Prehistory* by **J V S Megaw** and **D A A Simpson** (Leicester University Press, 1979), both of which present narrative accounts. For summaries of the changing environment during prehistoric times see *The Environment of Early Man in the British Isles* by

John Evans (Elek, 1975), and *The Environment in British Prehistory* edited by **Ian Simmons** and **Michael Tooley** (Duckworth, 1981). For prehistoric farming see *The Farming of Prehistoric Britain* by **Peter Fowler** (Cambridge University Press, 1983). On society and politics see *The Social Foundations of Prehistoric Britain* by **Richard Bradley** (Longman, 1984). *Current Archaeology* is a lively magazine focusing on recent finds and excavations published six times a year (available on subscription from 9 Nassington Road, London NW3 2TX).

JOINING IN

The enjoyment of visiting ancient monuments can be increased by joining **English Heritage** *(PO Box 43, Ruislip, Middlesex HA4 0XW)*, **Heritage in Wales** *(Cadw—Welsh Historic Monuments, Brunel House, 2 Fitzalan Road, Cardiff CF2 1UY)*, or the **Friends of Scottish Monuments,** *20 Brandon Street, Edinburgh EH3 5RA*. Members receive concessionary or free entry to guardianship sites, newsletters, information about special site visits and details of forthcoming events.

Guided walks around archaeological monuments are becoming increasingly popular, especially in National Parks and popular tourist areas. Details are usually available from Tourist Information Centres.

The Prehistoric Society is the main national society concerned with prehistory. It organises excursions and field trips to sites in Britain and abroad, holds lectures and meetings at which recent discoveries are described, issues an annual volume of *Proceedings* and distributes a *Newsletter*. Details are available by writing to **The Prehistoric Society,** *c/o 36 Great Russell Street, London WC1B 3PP*.

Local archaeological societies flourish in many areas. Most organise lectures and excursions, but some also undertake fieldwork, the recording of archaeological sites and excavations. A few are also concerned with the conservation of archaeological monuments. Your local reference library should have details of the societies in your area.

The **Council for British Archaeology,** *112 Kennington Road, London SE11 6RE* publishes a calendar of excavations, courses and holidays in its bi-monthly magazine *British Archaeological News*, available by subscription. Don't be put off from trying to join an excavation or survey because of inexperience. A wide range of skills and interests can find an application in archaeological work.

GLOSSARY

Avenue. Two parallel lines of standing stones, or a pair of parallel banks, defining a pathway or line of approach to a ceremonial monument. Possibly a processional way.

Bank barrow. Long low bank of soil and stones, sometimes with side ditches, of late Neolithic date. Possibly the focus of ceremonies which involved walking up and down the length of the monument.

Berm. Flat area between a ditch and an adjacent earthwork (eg barrow, bank, etc).

Broch. Circular tower with dwelling in the centre and rooms and passages within its stone walls. Constructed during the later Iron Age in northern Scotland.

Cairn. Heap of stones, often covering a burial, either gathered specially to build a mound or incidentally as a result of clearing fields.

Causewayed camp. Neolithic settlement and/or ceremonial site bounded by one or more rings of discontinuous ditches with a continuous bank on the inside broken only by entrances.

Cist. Stone-lined grave, usually rectangular in plan. Sometimes covered by a barrow.

Clyde-Carlingford long barrow. Rectangular stone mound covering slab-built chamber containing human remains (see **long barrow**).

Corbelling. Method of roofing which involves making successive layers of stone project forward over the preceding course until only a small gap is left which can be covered by a single slab to complete the roof.

Cotswold-Severn long barrow. Trapezoidal mound; chamber with front and side entrances (see **long barrow**).

Counterscarp bank. Small bank on the outer (downslope) edge of a defensive ditch.

Cove. Setting of upright stones, usually forming three sides of a square, found inside late Neolithic henges or near stone circles.

Cup-marks. Rock carvings comprising hemispherical depressions cut into a flat surface. When surrounded by pecked rings or other designs they are called **cup-and-ring marks**.

Cursus. Long narrow rectangular enclosure bounded by a bank and external ditch. Middle and late Neolithic in date. Used for ceremonial activities, possibly including processions.

Developed passage grave. Large round mound of earth and/or stones covering a central stone chamber which is approached from the outside of the mound through a long narrow passage.

Disc barrow. Small low mound with wide berm, enclosed by an outer ditch.

Dun. Scottish name for a small fort or fortified dwelling. The defences usually comprise massive stone walls. Mostly Iron Age and Romano-British in date, although some continued to be occupied into early Christian times.

Earthen long barrow. Long trapezoidal mound of earth and rubble covering burials contained within a wooden chamber (see **long barrow**).

Fieldsystem. A group of fields arranged for convenience of use, usually accessible from one another via gateways or droveways.

Forecourt. Semicircular area at the higher, wider end of a long barrow in which rituals were performed.

Henge. Large circular enclosure, sometimes containing a stone circle, characteristically bounded by a large bank with an internal ditch. Late Neolithic and early Bronze Age in date. Mostly used for ceremonial purposes.

Hillfort. Settlement situated on a hilltop which is defended by one or more lines of ramparts constructed from earth and stone. Hillfort building began in the north and west of Britain about 800BC, and continued down to the Roman Conquest.

Horns. Projections sticking out from the end of a long barrow, usually from the higher, wider end flanking the forecourt.

Hut circle. Stone foundations of a round house or building. These foundations usually supported a wooden superstructure.

Inhumation. Burial of complete unburnt corpse.

Linear earthwork. Substantial bank and ditch forming a major boundary between two adjacent landholdings. Most are of late Bronze Age and Iron Age date.

Long barrow. Roughly rectangular or wedge-shaped mound of earth and/or stones, sometimes bounded by a dry-stone wall or **peristalith**, which contains one or more stone or wooden chambers in which human bodies were buried. Mostly middle Neolithic in date, a number of regional traditions of long barrow building can be identified: for instance the Cotswold-Severn tradition, the earthen long barrow tradition and the Clyde-Carlingford tradition. See individual entries in glossary.

Lynchet. Bank of soil which accumulates against a boundary or fence as a result of the down-slope movement of soil during cultivation.

Oppidum. Large, regularly organised settlement of late Iron Age date, sometimes bounded by substantial earthworks but usually situated on or near a trading route (eg a river or port) rather than in a highly defensible position.

Orthostat. Large stone set upright to form part of the wall of a chamber within a long barrow.

Palisade. Fence or wall made of upright wooden posts set in the ground.

Peristalith. Ring of standing stones around a burial mound, usually forming a monumental kerb.

Portal dolmen. Small early Neolithic tomb comprising a rectangular chamber defined by three uprights set in an H-shaped formation at the front, a single upright at the back and a large capstone supported by the uprights. A low circular mound sometimes surrounded the chamber.

Radiocarbon dating. See page 9.

Revetment. A facing, usually of turf, wood or stone, designed to prevent the collapse of a mound or bank.

Ring cairn. A low unbroken bank of stones surrounding a circular area in the centre which was used for burial. Early Bronze Age in date.

Round barrow. Circular mound of earth and/or stone covering one or more burials (inhumations or cremations). Late Neolithic and Bronze Age in date. Sometimes called a 'tumulus' on Ordnance Survey maps.

Simple passage grave. Small circular mound of earth and/or stones covering a small stone chamber accessible from the outside of the mound via a short passage. The chamber was used to contain burials. Early to middle Neolithic in date.

Standing stone. Large block of stone, usually roughly rectangular in cross section, set upright to mark a cemetery or, when associated with a stone circle, a significant alignment of some kind. Mostly early to middle Bronze Age in date.

Stone circle. Ring of upright stones used for ritual and ceremonial purposes. Mostly late Neolithic and early Bronze Age in date. Some regional variations in design can be recognised.

Stone row. Line of three or more upright stones. Probably used to mark significant alignments or ceremonial way.

Trapezoidal. Four sided, with neither pair of sides parallel.

Tumulus. See **round barrow.**

INDEX

Page references to colour photographs/illustrations appear in **bold.**

A

Achnabreck, *Strathclyde* 110
Ackling Dyke, *Dorset* 24
Addington Long Barrow, *Kent* 51
Addington Moor Group, *West Yorkshire* 94
Afton Down, *Isle of Wight* 49
Aldworth, *Berkshire* 49
Almsworthy Stone Circle, *Somerset* 35
Amberley Camp, *Gloucestershire* 27
Arbor Low, *Derbyshire* 86–7
Arthur's Stone, *Hereford and Worcester* 74
Ashen Hill Barrow Cemetery, *Somerset* 35
Ash Hill Long Barrow, *Lincolnshire* 81
Auchagallon Stone Circle, *Strathclyde* 102
Avebury Area, *Wiltshire* 22–3
Avebury Museum, *Wiltshire* 22
Avebury Ring, *Wiltshire* **19,** 23
Aveline's Hole, *Somerset* 25

B

Badbury Rings, *Dorset* 24
Balbirnie Stone Circle, *Fife* 102–3
Balfarg Henge, *Fife* 102
Ballygowan Rocks, *Strathclyde* 110
Ballymeanock Standing Stones, *Strathclyde* 111

Bant's Cairn, *Scilly* 24, **37**
Barclodiad y Gawres, *Gwynedd* 56, **58,** 66
Barnfield Gravel Pit, *Kent* 52
Bee Low, *Derbyshire* 86
Belas Knap, *Gloucestershire* 25
Berkshire Ridgeway, *Oxfordshire* 44–5
Birkrigg Common, *Cumbria* 90
Boscawen-un, *Cornwall* 34
Bosiliack, *Cornwall* 33
Brats Hill, *Cumbria* 93
Brenig Valley Archaeological Trail, *Clwyd* 56
Bridestones, *Cheshire/ Staffordshire* 90
Bridgend, *Strathclyde* 111
British Camp, *Hereford and Worcester* 74–5
Broch of Gurness, *Orkney* 115
Bron-y-foel Isaf, *Gwynedd* 63
Bryncelli Ddu, *Gwynedd* 61, 66
Bull Ring, *Derbyshire* 87
Buluachraig, *Strathclyde* 110
Bulwarks, *Gloucestershire* 27
Burrough Hill, *Leicestershire* 75
Butser Hill Experimental Iron Age Farm, *Hampshire* **40,** 46

C

Caer y Twr, *Gwynedd* 67
Cairnbaan, *Strathclyde* 110
Cairnholy, *Dumfries and Galloway* **78,** 103
Cairnpapple Hill, *Lothian* 103
Callanish, *Western Isles* **79,** 104
Camster Long, *Highland* 104
Camster Round, *Highland* 104
Camulodunum, *Essex* 46
Cana, *North Yorkshire* 92
Capel Garmon Long Barrow, *Gwynedd* **58,** 61

Carn Euny, *Cornwall* 34
Carn Gluze, *Cornwall* 33
Carn Meini, *Dyfed* 69
Carreg Coitan, *Dyfed* 68
Castellhenllys, *Dyfed* 69
Castleheads, *Cumbria* 96
Castle Rigg Stone Circle, *Cumbria* 90–1
Cathole Cave, *West Glamorgan* 70
Cerrig Duon, *Powys* 62
Cerrig y Gof, *Dyfed* 68
Cheddar Gorge, *Somerset* 25
Chesters Broch, *Lothian* 105
Chestnuts Long Barrow, *Kent* 51
Chilton, *Oxfordshire* 49
Chun, *Cornwall* 33
Chun Castle, *Cornwall* 34
Chysauster, *Cornwall* 34
Cissbury, *West Sussex* 47
Clava Cairns, *Highland* 105
Clegyr Boia, *Dyfed* 69
Clickhimin Broch, *Shetland* 106
Cnoc Freiceadain, *Highland* 106
Colchester, *Essex* 46
Coldrum Long Barrow, *Kent* 51
Coome Hill Camp, *East Sussex* 47
Copt Hill Round Barrow, *Tyne and Wear* 91
Corndon Hill, *Shropshire* 84
Corrimony, *Highland* 107
Cotswolds (Central), *Gloucestershire* 26–7
Countless Stones, *Kent* 52
Creswell Crags, *Derbyshire* 75
Crickley Hill, *Gloucestershire* 28
Cullerlie Stone Circle, *Grampian* 107

D

Danebury, *Hampshire* 48
Deerleap Wood Round Barrow, *Surrey* 48

Devil's Arrows, North Yorkshire 77, 92
Devil's Dyke, *Hertfordshire* 54
Din Dryfol, *Gwynedd* 66
Doddington Moor, *Northumberland* 92
Dod Law Fort, *Northumberland* 92
Dragon Hill, *Oxfordshire* 45
Druids' Circle, *Gwynedd* 63
Duggleby Howe, *North Yorkshire* 97
Dunadd, *Strathclyde* 110
Dun Beag, *Highland* 108
Dun Carloway Broch, *Western Isles* 108
Dunmallet, *Cumbria* 96
Dun Mor, *Highland* 108
Durrington Walls, *Wiltshire* 28
Dyffryn Ardudwy Long Barrow, *Gwynedd* 63

E

East Aquhorties Stone Circle, *Grampian* 109
Eildon Hill, *Lothian* 105
Eskdale Moor, *Cumbria* 93

F

Ffridd Faldwyn, *Powys* 64
Fingal's Cauldron Seat, *Strathclyde* 113
Five Barrows, *Isle of Wight* 49
Five Barrows, *Northumberland* 93
Five Kings, *Northumberland* 93
Flag Fen, *Cambridgeshire* **60,** 76
Foeldrygarn, *Dyfed* 69
Foel Fenlli, *Clwyd* 64

G

Gib Hill, *Derbyshire* 86
Glebe Cairn, *Strathclyde* 111
Gors-fawr, *Dyfed* 69
Gough's Cave, *Somerset* 25
Graig Lwyd Axe Factory, *Gwynedd* 63
Grassington, *North Yorkshire* 94
Green Low, *Derbyshire* 86
Green Slack Group, *West Yorkshire* 94
Grimes Graves, *Norfolk* 76
Grim's Ditches, *Berkshire/Oxfordshire* 49
Grimspound, *Devon* 29
Grubstones Stone Circle, *West Yorkshire* 94
Grymes' Dyke, *Essex* 46
Gwernvale Long Barrow, *Powys* 65

H

Hambledon Hill, *Dorset* 29
Harold's Stones, *Gwent* 65
Hengistbury Head, *Dorset* 29
Hetty Pegler's Tump, *Gloucestershire* 26
High Close, *North Yorkshire* 94
Highdown Hill, *West Sussex* 50
High Rocks, *East Sussex/Kent* 54
Hob Hurst's House, *Derbyshire* 86
Hod Hill, *Dorset* 29
Hoe Hill Long Barrow, *Lincolnshire* 81
Holy Austin Rock, *Staffordshire* 82
Holy Island, *Gwynedd* 66—7
Horncliffe Stone Circle, *West Yorkshire* 94
Hunsbury Camp, *Northamptonshire* 81
Hurlers, *Cornwall* 30
Hutton Moor, *North Yorkshire* 92

I

Ilkley Moor, *West Yorkshire* 94
Innisidgen, *Scilly* 24
Isbister, *Orkney* 114
Ivinghoe Beacon, *Buckinghamshire* 50

J

Jacob's Knoll, *Gloucestershire* 27
Jarlshof, *Shetland* **78**, 109

K

Kilham Long Barrow, *Humberside* 98
Kilmartin Valley, *Strathclyde* 110—11
Kilmichael Glassary, *Strathclyde* 110
King Arthur's Cave, *Hereford and Worcester* 82
King Arthur's Round Table, *Cumbria* 95—6
King's Men, *Oxfordshire* 53, 57
King Stone, *Oxfordshire* 53
Kinver Camp, *Staffordshire* 82
Kits Coty, *Kent* 52
Knowlton Henges, *Dorset* 30

L

Laggangairn Standing Stones, *Dumfries and Galloway* 112
Langdale Pikes, *Cumbria* 93
Lanyon Quoit, *Cornwall* 33

Lea Green, *North Yorkshire* 94
Lexden Dyke, *Essex* 46
Lexden Tumulus, *Essex* 46
Little Kits Coty, *Kent* 52
Little Meg, *Cumbria* 95
Llanbedr Church, *Gwynedd* 63
Lligwy Burial Chamber, *Gwynedd* 66
Llyn Cerrig Bach, *Gwynedd* 67
Loanhead Stone Circle, *Grampian* 112
Long Meg and Her Daughters, *Cumbria* 95
Long Stone, *Gloucestershire* **20**, 27
Low Longrigg Stone Circles, *Cumbria* 93

M

Machrie Moor, *Strathclyde* 113
Maeshowe, *Orkney* 114
Maiden Castle, *Dorset* 31, **37**
Mam Tor, *Derbyshire* 83
Mayborough Henge, *Cumbria* 96
Medway Area, *Kent* 51—2
Men-an-Tol, *Cornwall* 33
Mendip Caves, *Somerset* 25
Merrivale, *Devon* 31
Merry Maidens, *Cornwall* 33—4
Michael Moorey's Hump, *Isle of Wight* 49
Mid Howe, *Orkney* 114
Minchinhampton Common, *Gloucestershire* 27
Minninglow, *Derbyshire* 87
Mitchell's Fold Stone Circle, *Shropshire* 84
Moel Arthur, *Clwyd* 64
Moel y Gaer, *Clwyd* 64
Mousa Broch, *Shetland* 113
Mulfra, *Cornwall* 33
Mynydd Preseli, *Dyfed* 68—9

N

Na Tri Shean, *Highland* 106
Nether Largie Barrow Cemetery, *Strathclyde* 111
Nether Largie Middle, *Strathclyde* 111
Nether Largie North, *Strathclyde* 111
Nether Largie South, *Strathclyde* 111
Nether Largie Standing Stones, *Strathclyde* 110
Nevern Valley, *Dyfed* 68—9
Nine Ladies Stone Circle, *Derbyshire* 87
Nine Maidens, *Cornwall* 32
Norton Fitzwarren, *Somerset* 32
Nympsfield Long Barrow, *Gloucestershire* 26

O

Oldbury Camp, *Kent* 52
Oldbury Rock Shelter, *Kent* 52
Old Oswestry Hillfort, *Shropshire* 84—5
Orkney 114—15
Oxton Camp, *Nottinghamshire* 85

P

Parc Cwm Long Barrow, *West Glamorgan* 70
Peak District (South), *Derbyshire* 86—7
Penrhosfeilw, *Gwynedd* **59**, 66
Penrith Area, *Cumbria* 95—6
Pentre Ifan, *Dyfed* 68
Penwith Area, *Cornwall* 33—4

Penycloddiau, *Clwyd* 64
Porlock Stone Circle, *Somerset* 35
Porth Hellick Down, *Scilly* 24
Presaddfed Burial Chamber, *Gwynedd* 66
Priddy Circles, *Somerset* 35
Priddy Nine Barrows, *Somerset* 35

R

Rhosybeddau, *Powys* 70
Ri Cruin Cairn, *Strathclyde* 111
Ridgeway, *Oxfordshire* 44—5
Ring of Brogar, *Orkney* 115
Rivock Group, *West Yorkshire* 94
Robin Hood's Pot, *Nottinghamshire* 85
Rollright Stones, *Oxfordshire* 53, **57**
Royston Grange Trail, *Derbyshire* 87
Rudston Area, *Humberside/North Yorkshire* 97—8
Rudston Monolith, *Humberside* 98
Rumps, *Cornwall* 36

S

St Catherine's Hill, *Hampshire* 53
St Lythans Long Barrow, *South Glamorgan* 71
Sanctuary, *Wiltshire* 23
Shalcombe Down, *Isle of Wight* 49
Silbury Hill, *Wiltshire* 23
Skara Brae, *Orkney* **80**, 115
Skirtful of Stones, *West Yorkshire* 94
Slad, *Hertfordshire* 54
Soldier's Grave, *Gloucestershire* 27
Somerset Levels Museum 36, **38**
South Peak District, *Derbyshire* 86—7
Stanton Drew, *Avon* 41
Stanton Moor, *Derbyshire* 87
Stanwick, *North Yorkshire* 98—9
Steinacleit Chambered Cairn, *Western Isles* 116
Stonehenge, *Wiltshire* **39**, 41, 69
Stones of Stenness, *Orkney* 115
Stoney Littleton, *Avon* 42
Sweetside, *North Yorkshire* 94

T

Temple Wood Stone Circle, *Strathclyde* 110
Thornborough Henges, *North Yorkshire* 99
Tinkinswood Long Barrow, *South Glamorgan* 71
Toots, *Gloucestershire* 27
Traprain Law, *Lothian* 105
Trefignath Long Barrow, *Gwynedd* 66
Trefignath Standing Stone, *Gwynedd* 66
Tre'r Ceiri, *Gwynedd* 72
Teryn Dinas, *Cornwall* 36
Trethevy Quoit, *Cornwall* **40**, 42
Trevelgue Head, *Cornwall* 36
Triple Dyke, *Essex* 46
Tunbridge Wells, *Kent* 54
Twelve Apostles, *West Yorkshire* 94
Ty Mawr Settlement, *Gwynedd* 66—7
Ty Newydd, *Gwynedd* 66

U

Uffington Castle, *Oxfordshire* 45
Uffington White Horse, *Oxfordshire* 44—5
Uley Bury, *Gloucestershire* 27
Unstan Chambered Cairn, *Orkney* 114

V

Victoria Cave, *North Yorkshire* **77**, 100

W

Warham Camp, *Norfolk* 88
Waulod's Bank, *Bedfordshire* 54
Wayland's Smithy Long Barrow, *Oxfordshire* 45
West Kennett Avenue, *Wiltshire* 23
West Kennett Long Barrow, *Wiltshire* **19**, 22—3
West Rudham Long Barrow, *Norfolk* 88
Wheathampstead, *Hertfordshire* 54
Whispering Knights, *Oxfordshire* 53
Whitefield's Tump, *Gloucestershire* 27
White Moss Stone Circles, *Cumbria* 93
Willerby Wold Long Barrow, *Humberside* 97—8
Willy Howe, *Humberside* 97
Windmill Hill, *Wiltshire* 22
Windmill Tump, *Gloucestershire* 27
Withypool Stone Circle, *Somerset* 35
Woldgate, *Humberside* 98
Wold Newton Barrow, *Humberside* 97
Woodhenge, *Wiltshire* 28
Wookey Hole, *Somerset* 25

Y

Yanwath Wood, *Cumbria* 96
Yeavering Bell, *Northumberland* 100
Y Gaer Fawr, *Dyfed* 72

Z

Zennor, *Cornwall* 33